Objects of Design

Objects of Design

from The Museum of Modern Art

Paola Antonelli

The Museum of Modern Art, New York

Produced by the Department of Publications,
The Museum of Modern Art

Edited by Harriet Schoenholz Bee
Design and composition by Gina Rossi
Production by Christina Grillo
Printed and bound by Dr. Cantz'sche Druckerei,
Ostfildern, Germany
Printed on 150 gsm Nopacoat Matt

Library of Congress Control Number: 2003103402
ISBN: 0–87070-696-9

Published by The Museum of Modern Art,
11 West 53 Street
New York, New York 10019
www.moma.org

Distributed in the United States and Canada by
D.A.P./Distributed Art Publishers, Inc., New York

Distributed outside the United States and Canada by
Thames & Hudson, Ltd., London

Front cover: Collage of various objects in the collection.
Back cover: Gaetano Pesce. Feltri Chair. 1986. Wool felt
and polyester resin, 50⅛ × 55⅛ × 28" (127.3 × 140 × 71.1 cm).
Manufacturer: Cassina, Italy. Gift of the manufacturer
Frontispiece: Ingo Maurer. Bulb Lamp. 1966. Chromium-
plated metal and glass, 11¾ × 7⅞" (30 × 20 cm). Gift of
the designer

Printed in Germany

Contents

Foreword

Objects of Design is the second installment, after *Envisioning Architecture* of 2002, in The Museum of Modern Art's three-volume series on the holdings of the Department of Architecture and Design, which reflect the Museum's extraordinary role in shaping the history of modern design.

Together with architecture, design was part of the Museum's composition from the very start, in accordance with Alfred H. Barr, Jr.'s Bauhaus-inspired vision of a new unity of the arts of our own time. Unlike architecture, however, design was not endowed with a leading theory for curators to embrace or rebel against. From Philip Johnson's first design exhibitions, *Objects: 1900 and Today* and *Machine Art*, in 1933 and 1934 respectively, to Peter Reed's recent show, *AUTObodies: speed, sport, transport*, an installation of six cars for the opening of MoMA QNS in 2002, the curators have dealt with virgin territory, establishing criteria for the modern ideal while asking those same objects for a confirmation of their empirical constructs. The intellectual power of their work and that of their colleagues can only be acknowledged after the fact, by contemplating the complexity, strength, imperfections, variety, and yet consistency of the collection of design objects.

The design collection of nearly 4,000 items, comprises objects as diverse as hair dryers, surfboards, chairs, microchips, and a helicopter. Bringing them all together recognizes not only the highest synthesis of function and beauty, but also the belief in the necessity to adhere to a design process that uses function as a generator of form.

This volume, structured and produced with passion by Paola Antonelli, could not have happened without the support and guidance of Terence Riley, The Philip Johnson Chief Curator, and the joint efforts of Ms. Antonelli's generous colleagues in the Department of Architecture and Design. Published at a moment in history when design is becoming more and more relevant as a cultural model in all spheres of human activity, it celebrates The Museum of Modern Art's enduring mission to support the art of our time.

Glenn D. Lowry, Director
The Museum of Modern Art

Preface

The design collection of The Museum of Modern Art has been formed over the course of seventy-five years by many curatorial voices. Among the Museum's curators, Philip Johnson, Eliot Noyes, Edgar Kaufmann, Jr., Mildred Constantine, Arthur Drexler, and others have played an important role in shaping the collection of design objects represented here, a modest selection from a total of 3,708 objects presently in the Museum's holdings. In addition to the individual eye and mind of the custodians of the Museum's collection, there is also a curious alchemy that a collection of objects manifests by its very existence, defining what might be termed its collective meaning. In this sense, individual objects may also be participants in the subsequent shaping of the collection in unpredictable, but critical, ways.

Inasmuch as many significant vectors might be seen to intersect within a single object, it is interesting to examine, for example, one of the very first design objects to be exhibited at The Museum of Modern Art: the Armchair with Adjustable Back (*Siège à dossier basculant*), designed in 1927 by Le Corbusier, Pierre Jeanneret, and Charlotte Perriand, and originally presented in Paris at the Salone d'Automne of 1929. This tubular-steel chair was also one of the first design objects to be acquired by the Museum, which exhibited it in the Museum's second design exhibition, *Machine Art,* in 1934. Now widely known as the Basculant Chair, it reflects many of the characteristics that later came to define the Museum's design collection as a critical and exclusive assembly, rather than encyclopedic and comprehensive.

One of the leading characteristics of the Museum's design collection is the idea that its design objects are part of larger visions within which they are best seen. As beautiful as they may be individually, design objects are considered to be more meaningful when they can be seen as part of idealized environments, and when they embody more than mere function. Many Americans had not seen the Paris debut of the Basculant Chair before it was shown at the Museum, but were perhaps aware of it because it was depicted in many periodicals of the time, along with other furniture by the same team of designers that furnished the interior of Le Corbusier's much-celebrated "machine for living in," the Villa Savoye. This famous house, which was exhibited in model form in the Museum's *Modern Architecture—International Exhibition* in 1932, was a paradigm for a radical new mode of habitation, and the Basculant Chair was one of its principal tools in the expression of modernism. Not surprisingly, as the design collection grew, the designers who had also created architectural environments were represented with greater frequency than others.

Implied by the rhetoric of Le Corbusier's well-known aphorism was the invocation of the aesthetics of the machine. With its chrome-plated tubular-steel structure, exposed springs, and pivoting back, the Basculant Chair adhered to the architect's planar, abstract architectural vocabulary. Following the lead of Le Corbusier and others, the Museum's curators believed that it was this expression of the machine aesthetic that bespoke the spirit of the age. Additionally, the acquisition of the Basculant Chair in 1934, expressed the Museum's critique of the streamlined styles of 1920s industrial design as well as of the machine motifs of Art Deco. The collection's continued omission of this popular style limits its encyclopedic character but preserves the memory of the important critical discussions that engaged the Museum in its early days.

The Basculant Chair not only expressed the machine metaphor, it was manufactured under mechanical conditions, that is, mass produced in a factory using the anonymous industrial techniques that distinguished modern furniture from Arts and Crafts objects. The means of production were intended to reduce costs and make such objects more widely accessible to a growing middle class. The hallmark of mass production so evident in the Basculant Chair influenced the growth of the design collection, perhaps more than any other characteristic. Again, this influence can be seen in terms of inclusion and exclusion. The focus on mass production excluded the extensive collecting of handmade objects (although there were some) as well as prototypes and luxury goods, which were rarely collected because they lacked compatibility with mass-produced objects.

Another important characteristic of the Basculant Chair is the fact that it was a traditional object—a chair. As those who have studied the design collection at any length can't help notice, among all the other design objects chairs play a particularly important role. Not only is the chair a traditional type of object, with over two thousand years of history, it is a type of object particularly loved by both designers and users. The reason for the enduring bond between the maker, the user, and the chair is less functional than empathic. If the chair were solely a functional object, one might have expected that its form could have been settled centuries ago. But the chair is more than just a place to rest. Like the human being, it has legs, arms, a seat, and a back. Furthermore, to accommodate us, it is human in size; it is, in fact, a mirror of ourselves, and despite its overt functional genesis it serves essentially as an expressive and subjective portrait of its maker and its prospective users.

Unlike photography, which the Museum has always considered a wholly modern art form, modern architecture and design have often involved the transformation of existing formal and functional types. Indeed, the 1933 exhibition *Objects: 1900 and Today* clearly demonstrated this point by pairing objects such as lamps, tables, and chairs, in a turn-of-the-century Art Nouveau style and a more severely abstract contemporary rendition. While a display of propellers and ball bearings in an art museum might have brought smiles to visitors' faces, the radical transformation of familiar and personal objects was often more challenging.

Today, as the influence of the machine wanes in an increasingly digital world, as it has over the past few decades, we see the center of gravity of the design collection beginning to shift. In the words of the contemporary author Italo Calvino, in "Lightness" (from *Six Essays for the Millennium*): "The heavy machines still exist, but now they obey the commands of weightless bits." So the challenge, then, while different in specifics, remains: to identify anew those objects that most clearly tell us about ourselves, the culture that produced them, and the world in which we aspire to live.

Terence Riley
The Philip Johnson Chief Curator
Department of Architecture and Design
The Museum of Modern Art, New York

Acknowledgments

The Museum of Modern Art's extraordinary collection of objects would not exist without the designers who created them and the donors who made their acquisition possible. The Museum has been the fortunate beneficiary of their generosity. A particular debt of gratitude is owed the Museum's Committee on Architecture and Design whose generous support has been responsible for countless acquisitions. Led by its present chairman, Museum trustee Patricia Phelps de Cisneros, the Committee has, over the years, also benefited from the leadership of such past chairmen as Philip Johnson, Lily Auchincloss, Edward Larrabee Barnes, and Marshall S. Cogan; they have all been committed to ensuring the growth and strength of the collection. Equally important have been the directors of the Department of Architecture and Design, who, along with their curators, have shaped the collection. There have been six directors since the department was established in 1932: Philip Johnson, Philip Goodwin, Eliot Noyes, Arthur Drexler, Stuart Wrede, and Terence Riley, the present chief curator. Each has left an outstanding legacy of exhibitions and acquisitions.

The Director of the Museum, Glenn D. Lowry, has been an enthusiastic supporter of the project since it was first proposed; Terence Riley, The Philip Johnson Chief Curator in the Department of Architecture and Design, has not only provided valuable support during the preparation of the publication but also an insightful preface that gives an historical understanding of collecting objects of design.

The outstanding quality of the photographic reproductions in this volume has been essential to its creation. It has been part of a two-and-a-half-year project to digitize the architecture and design collection, generously funded by the Andrew W. Mellon Foundation. The digital photography was coordinated by Luna Imaging of Culver City, California; and I am grateful to Michael Ester, Maria Mapes, and Drake Zabriskie of Luna for their fine work and commitment to the project. Angelica Zander Rudenstine, Senior Advisor, Museums and Conservation, at the Mellon Foundation was instrumental in providing the funding for the project. From the outset, she showed extraordinary foresight and championed the effort to make this virtual collection available to a wide audience.

The Museum's Imaging Services Department coordinated the photography with Luna. I wish to thank Mikki Carpenter, Director of Imaging Services; Holly Boerner, Assistant to the Director; Erik Landsberg, Head of Collections Imaging; and Thomas Griesel, Collections Photographer, who have given valuable technical expertise to this endeavor. A special acknowledgment goes to Angela Lange, Curatorial Assistant in the Department of Painting and Sculpture, whose contribution to this book went well beyond her normal professional duties; she served as the model for the Fortuny y Madrazo gown shown in this book.

In the Department of Publications, I am grateful to Michael Maegraith, Publisher; Lawrence Allen, Publications Manager; Marc Sapir, Director of Production; Christina Grillo, Assistant Production Manager, whose patience and gentle pushing have kept the book on schedule; and Gina Rossi, Senior Book Designer, whose beautiful publication design is a fitting tribute to the objects. It has been both an honor and a delight to work with Harriet S. Bee, Editorial Director, and modern editor *par excellence*, whose editorial insight and special knowledge of the Architecture and Design department have given this volume the straight spine and the narrative pace that it called for.

Finally, I would like to thank the members of the staff of the Department of Architecture and Design, who have worked so well in concert to create this publication. I especially thank those colleagues who contributed texts to this volume: Terence Riley; Peter Reed, Curator, who generously provided invaluable counsel on the main essay; Bevin Cline, Assistant Curator, Research and Collections; Tina di Carlo, Curatorial Assistant for Research and Collections; Christian Larsen, Senior Cataloguer; and former colleagues Matilda McQuaid, Christopher Mount, and Luisa Lorch. In addition, essential research conducted by Bryan Kessler, Cataloguer, proved invaluable to all of the contributors; and special thanks are owed for all the hours of work and additional research done by interns Melissa Kahn, Geaninne Gutierrez, and Mesve Vardar. And last but not least, Rachel Judlowe, Nobi Nakanishi, and Curbie Oestreich Cohen have been the crucial support staff facilitating the entire process. I am deeply indebted to them and to all who played significant roles in the realization of this project.

Paola Antonelli, Curator
Department of Architecture and Design

Objects of Design

Paola Antonelli

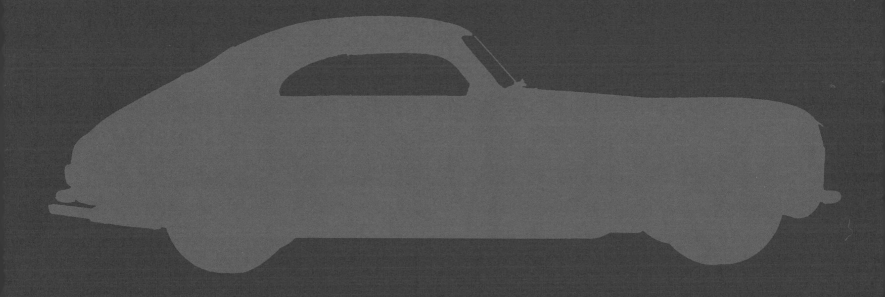

The Museum of Modern Art's collection of design objects represents the foremost assemblage of its kind in the field of twentieth-century design. While several other excellent collections exist in the United States and elsewhere—some larger and more encyclopedic, others smaller and specially focused—the Museum's authoritative curatorial choices over nearly seventy-five years have done nothing less than establish modern industrial design among the arts and provide a premise against which others must measure themselves. The Museum's collection of design objects and textiles now includes 3,708 objects, the oldest a silk brocade from the seventeenth century and the most recent a felt fabric designed by the Dutch artist Claudy Jongstra in 2001. The collection ranges among diverse types of objects, materials, and sizes, from a helicopter (the biggest item in the collection) to eleven microchips (the smallest). As expected in a design collection, a significant percentage of the objects are chairs; among the other objects are household appliances, cars, office equipment and furnishings, sports equipment, a Paris métro entrance, a ball bearing, various tools, a glider nose, and a drinking straw.

This narrative traces the history of the objects in concert with that of the growth of the Museum's Department of Architecture and Design. In the process, it examines the evolution of the ideas that form the backbone of the collection: the meaning of modern design, the formation of the collection, its guiding principles, its periods of growth and change, its acquisition policies, its influence on designers internationally, and its relevance today.

Modern Design in a Museum of Modern Art

The term *modern* does not refer to an historical phenomenon but, rather, a spirit in tune with its own time. The Museum of Modern Art was created in 1929 for the express purpose of furthering and supporting the art of its own time, for "encouraging and developing the study of modern arts and the application of such arts to manufacture and practical life."[1] The idea of the Museum's founders, and especially its founding director, Alfred H. Barr, Jr., was to have a museum concerned with all the arts of their own day, and modern design was included among those arts from the outset.

The Museum's very first acquisitions in design were a group of more than a hundred industrial objects shown in its second exhibition of design, *Machine Art*, in 1934. The organizers of the show were Barr and Philip Johnson, whose 1932 *Modern Architecture—International Exhibition*, the Museum's first architecture show, in collaboration with Henry-Russell Hitchcock, had defined modern architecture in a way that was to have a lasting influence throughout the twentieth century.

Johnson's idea for a comparable design exhibition was formed as early as 1932, when he proposed to the Museum's trustees an exhibition of art in industry, which they did not approve.[2] The following year, Johnson presented the Museum's first design exhibition, one that was able to achieve a nod from the trustees: an installation that included contemporary objects inspired by the machine but was not entirely limited to them. Already a strong declaration of intent, *Objects: 1900 and Today* was a display of delicate Art Nouveau and Jugendstil objects juxtaposed with stern machinelike objects. The majority of the objects selected were borrowed from the houses of trustees, and many came from the home of Johnson's mother. The comparative exercise made the subject more acceptable to the Museum's trustees and public alike.

With *Machine Art,* shortly thereafter, Johnson surprised the new Museum's audience with a three-story display of machine-made objects, from propeller blades to coils and springs, manufactured laboratory appliances and working tools, household objects, and furniture. Set on white pedestals and platforms and against white walls, the decontextualized objects were installed with the same focus and drama that was reserved for sculpture.[3]

Machine Art provided a great leap forward. Although it was not the first time people could contemplate everyday objects in a museum setting, these were not the usual decorative arts or modern household items.[4] The jolting elevation of a ball bearing to the stature of art and its acquisition into a collection of modern art had the strength and the authority of a manifesto. While the Museum's painting and sculpture collection was at first relatively conservative, the design collection had a brazen start.[5] As Johnson put it several years earlier, at age twenty-five, in a letter to Barr: "What I want most to do is to be influential and if there's a method why not learn it."[6] *Modern Architecture—International Exhibition* and *Machine Art* were warnings of what was to follow.

The origins of this bold attitude can be traced initially to Barr's undergraduate courses at Princeton with the medievalist Charles Rufus Morey, who had taught him to appreciate the "synthesis of the principal medieval visual arts as a record of a period of civilization."[7] Barr aspired to attain a similarly encompassing synthesis of the arts of today, first in a unique course in modern art that he taught at Wellesley College, and soon after with his groundbreaking vision for the Museum. At Wellesley, as an Associate Professor, Barr taught a modern art course that included theater, music, and industrial design. In 1927, he visited the Bauhaus in Dessau, the school originally founded in Weimar by Walter Gropius in 1919 dedicated to gathering together the arts of sculpture, painting, handicraft, and the crafts "to achieve in a new architecture, *the unification of all training in art and design.* The ultimate, if distant, goal of the Bauhaus is the *collective work of art*—the Building—in which no barrier exists between the structural and the decorative arts."[8] This ideal resonated with Barr to the extent that he later acknowledged

The Museum's first design exhibition, *Objects: 1900 and Today*, 1933

the Bauhaus, as well as Morey, as an inspiration for the shaping of the Museum.

Barr and Johnson had met in 1929, six months before the Museum opened, at Johnson's sister Theodate's graduation from Wellesley, where their conversation began a friendship based on their shared cultural interests, their daring intellectual passion for modern contemporary art, and their enthusiasm for the machine age and the promise of a new unity of the arts. Barr's acknowledgment of the importance of design was unabashed, as can be seen in his original text for the Museum's opening brochure, where he wrote: "In time the Museum would probably expand beyond the narrow limits of painting and sculpture in order to include departments devoted to drawings, prints, and photography, typography, the arts of design in commerce and industry, architecture (a collection of *projets* and *maquettes*), stage designing, furniture and the decorative arts. Not the least important collection might be the *filmotek*, a library of films."[9] The founding trustees, however, cautiously formulated this declaration differently in the final text: "In time the Museum would expand ... to include other phases of modern art."[10]

Johnson did not have any formal training in design or architecture at the time of his graduation from Harvard in 1930, with a degree in philosophy; he later returned to get a degree in architecture in 1943. But he had learned about buildings by taking a grand tour of Europe with Hitchcock in 1929, which, no doubt on the advice of his friend Barr, also included a stop at the Bauhaus. When it came to evaluating design and architecture, he relied on his sharp instincts and exceptional synthetic skills. In his 1933 introduction to *Objects: 1900 and Today*, Johnson articulated one of the defining principles of modern design, its deep connection with architecture: "Today industrial design is functionally motivated and follows the same principles as modern architecture: machine-like simplicity, smoothness of surface, avoidance of ornament. . . . It is perhaps the most fundamental contrast between the two periods of design that in 1900 the Decorative Arts possessed a style of their own, independent of the architecture of the time, whereas today the discipline of modern architecture has become so broad that there can be no subcategory as that of the decorative arts."[11] In Johnson's view of the visual arts, design was, if not on a par with architecture, at least its direct emanation.[12] The interdependence between design and architecture effectively

freed the realm of objects from its single-minded ties to form and, by assigning to function an equal importance, positioned it in the light of a critical theory based on the balance between means and goals, with beauty among the highest of these. This concept is engrained in the very definition of the architecture and design department and has been reinforced and adapted by the thoughts of several generations of curators. Even though the department was briefly divided into separate branches between 1940 and 1948, the unity of architecture and design as professed in the European modern movement remained among the ideals of the Museum's design curators, many of whom have themselves been architects.

In 1944, for instance, the Museum's executive administrator (and later director) René d'Harnoncourt and the architect Serge Chermayeff declared that the revolution in the design of the domestic environment brought about by modern architects had generated a whole new approach in the design of furniture: "The development of modern furniture has always been closely related to the evolution of modern architecture. . . . The recognition that a house is essentially a problem of interrelated functions made it necessary to think of individual pieces of home equipment as components

The Museum's second design exhibition, *Machine Art*, 1934

of a unit of effective living space rather than as individual esthetic and technical problems."[13] This echo of Le Corbusier's definition of the house as a "machine for living in," and an interest in the works of certain architects, for example, Ludwig Mies van der Rohe and Alvar Aalto, inspired the early acquisition of modern architects' furniture, such as the so-called Basculant Chair (1927), designed by Le Corbusier, Pierre Jeanneret, and Charlotte Perriand. In the 1960s, when architecture took a new turn in an attempt to move beyond the dogma of modernism, the relationship between design and architecture evolved into an even more mature partnership. Design, more agile in scale and less subject to intense intellectual scrutiny, not only actively contributed technical knowledge to architectural research, but also provided it with an array of possible new conceptual departure points that could take into account the new circumstances of a changed world. This new integration of architecture and design, in which design was able to provide some of the paradigms for mastering and inhabiting space, was celebrated in the 1972 exhibition *Italy: The New Domestic Landscape*, which was filled with objects of environmental design and dense with adaptable environments with the potential to alter human behavior.

Moreover, in the 1960s and 1970s, the advent of the influential French philosophical theory known as post-structuralism, which devalued reality in favor of a universe of relative meanings, brought modern architecture and design even closer in their common search for truth. Together, they found it in alertness and continuous adaptation, and in their resolve to adhere to a process centered on clarity of purpose, no matter how anachronistic. These solid values have regained currency today, and proven the validity and timelessness of the modern ideal.

A Collection of Ideas

At the time of the founding of the Museum, the terms *modern* and *contemporary* coin-

Le Corbusier (Charles-Édouard Jeanneret), Pierre Jeanneret, and Charlotte Perriand. Armchair with Adjustable Back (Basculant Chair). 1927. Chrome-plated tubular steel and black canvas, 26⅛ × 25⅝ × 26" (66.3 × 65 × 66 cm). The Museum of Modern Art, New York. Gift of Thonet Brothers, Inc.

cided effortlessly within Barr's vision of a museum of, in his words, the Art of Our Time. By trial and error, over seven decades, the Museum's curators have sought to distill a timeless ideal of beauty and meaning from different circumstances, all the while revising and perfecting the initial paradigm. They have searched widely, among inexpensive everyday objects and prohibitive one-off pieces alike, in catalogues, in hardware stores, and in private collections. They have reassessed their ideas to meet changing historical and technical conditions, and they have made discoveries and mistakes. Each curatorial team's choices have been celebrated, amended, and revised. The result of this collective, sometimes subjective, effort is not just an accumulation of objects but a collection of ideas supported by objects.

Several of the themes developed in the collection by the different curators are still a lively aspect of discussion within the department. Advanced by the curators at different times, often in the form of exhibitions, their theoretical strength has proven timeless, and to this day they serve as an inspiration for new acquisitions. Some of these themes are connected to a specific period, for instance,

the turn of the century, the 1920s and 1930s, or the aftermath of World War II, and yet they are constantly rediscussed and extended. Others, such as the interest in the potential of advanced materials, machine components, and the interrelationships among products, markets, corporations, and the modern ideal are in constant evolution. In the search for modern design, the curators have used various paths of exploration that have enabled them to approach the collection methodically. Some of these paths have crystallized in strong ideas within the collection.

These themes are not only the spine of the collection but also of this volume, which describes the history of the collection as a history of ideas. The illustrations, grouped into nine thematic sections, open with Turning Points, a description of the productive cultural atmosphere that prepared the way for modern design, some eighty years before the founding of the Museum. Dedicated to the consequences for design of the Industrial Revolution, this section examines the embryonic tenets that became the focus of the collection by celebrating the efforts by such historical figures as William Morris, Charles Rennie Mackintosh, and Josef Hoffmann, to name a few, to direct and rationalize, or oppose, the brand-new industrial world's exuberance toward a higher moral and aesthetic purpose. It zeroes in on the connections between the modern ideal and the differences among classes, and on the relationship between modern design and manufacturing processes. In this way, it sets the tone for The Modern Ideal, which explains the characteristics by which the collection is best known. The Modern Ideal represents the moment of highest synthesis of the arts, which so inspired Barr and Johnson, that in which architecture and design are joined not only in theory but also in practice. The several recognizable masterpieces in this group, designed by, among others, Ludwig Mies van der Rohe, Le Corbusier, and Marianne Brandt, identify the core of the collection. In addition, hundreds of other objects provide the collection with a broader syntax and thus make it accessible.

Many of these less well-known objects are described in Machine Art, Useful Objects, and Good Design, sections that discuss the interdependence of beauty, function, and process. Yet, in each section, one variable of the equation of modernism is emphasized. In Machine Art, a celebration of "the splendid inherent beauty of industrial engineering," pure machine-made objects are judged according to aesthetic criteria.[14] In Useful Objects, perfect functionality makes the objects beautiful. Objects are seen through a critical lens, which examines their function and the soundness of the design approach. Both methods arrive at the same conclusions, but the different paths represent different priorities and lines of attack that have been useful to curators at different moments in history. Both critical stances are still valuable and suitable today, as is the consideration displayed in the section dealing with Good Design.

In Good Design, the ideal developed by modern architects and designers and celebrated by curators is given an everyday context and transformed into suggestions for modern living. Filling the gap between the Museum and people's homes, it offers tasteful consumption and living styles, and it places the modern ideal within a more complete narrative reality by providing people with suggestions for products available in stores and with parables for modern lifestyles. It was particularly strong in the 1950s, in a series of exhibitions that presented a selection based on eye-appeal, function, construction, and price, with emphasis on the first.

Good Design for Industry and Mind over Matter are two discrete topics that represent different facets of the complex design enterprise, in particular, manufacture and distribution. Good Design for Industry covers the production of the few companies that, in the curators' views, have remained true to the modern ideal—in their corporate image, the style of their showrooms, their advertising, and the products they have released over the years. Mind over Matter, on the other hand, delineates the importance of materials and techniques, the valuable inspiration they provide designers and engineers, and their relationship with the development of several ideas, comfort and beauty among them. A curatorial theme introduced in recent years, the study of advanced materials and technological innovations, encompasses objects acquired earlier, revealing the ever-present interest in technology as a tool for design excellence.

Modern Nature features design ideas found in nature, as adapted by designers at different times and as transformed through technological innovations. The organic quality of these objects, not always reflected by literal naturalistic shapes, lies in the effort to attain a complete and seamless integration of form and function.

The section titled The Object Transformed closes the book with a collection of idiosyncratic approaches to design, which often play on the modern ideal. Here are the dissident design voices, apparent paradoxes, ironic commentary, risky experiments, and humor—all bent to the ideal of excellence as the ultimate guiding idea of the collection.

What Is Modern Design?

The Museum's idea of modern design goes beyond the stereotypical stylistic traits commonly attributed to modernism. The modern ideal is distinct from modernism. The innovative and reductionist beauty of the objects from the *Machine Art* show, indeed, exemplified the perfection that the machine as a form-giving tool could afford; nonetheless, since the beginning, modern design under the aegis of the machine was seen as the carrier of the solid human values of truth, objectivity, and honesty. In addition to a unity of the arts celebrated by Barr and Johnson, the machine also carried the promise of deep social change through *organic design,* a term derived from the idea of the organic interplay of function, technology, and form: "Since it is the aim of organic design to provide people with better tools for living, its application presupposes an attitude of responsibility toward society sustained by a professional code of ethics comparable to those of science and medicine."[15]

Therefore, the design collection's essence lies not in a formalist criterion but, rather, a deontological one. The machine stands as a higher authority to which the designer responds, and it commands a higher sense of purpose and responsibility, for it guides the artist to a human-centered, rather than object-centered, kind of design. Modern design is also distinguished by its attention to the preliminary phases of the design process, the gathering of information about the needs and functions to be addressed. Edgar Kaufmann, Jr.'s 1946 article, "What Is Modern Industrial Design*?*" explained: "In modern design each problem is considered to carry the germ of its own solution—full comprehension of the needs to be fulfilled will indicate the form of the design. Although as in every art expressive exaggeration is used, arbitrary shapes chosen without relation to the problem are looked on as weakness, not strength. The responsibility of a modern designer thus becomes understanding his problem as thoroughly as he can and solving it as directly as he can. Modern designers do not wish to overcome conditions; they wish to meet them. Functions, materials, techniques, the environment and psychology of users—these are not to be circumvented or forced, they are guides to right design… Sales are episodes in the careers of designed objects. Use is the first consideration, production and distribution second… In the hands of a great artist, the resulting design will be beautiful. In all hands, modern industrial design must remain ethical according to its code; abandoning this, it becomes mere promotional trickery as machine-carved 'Chippendale' chairs or 'streamlined' bathroom scales."[16]

Exhibition, *Useful Objects in Wartime under $10*, 1941–42

Deploring style for the sake of style—or for the sake of commerce—has become a trademark of the collection and resulted in several exclusions, the first of them being Art Deco and the streamline manner, and one of the most recent being postmodernism, in the instances where it has become an easy stylistic trick. The current curatorial choices, while not explicitly excluding whole groups of objects or designers, still privilege objects whose form is generated from within. The lack of prejudice against form helped the modern ideal withstand the crisis of modernism in the 1960s. Whether the objects were sofas in the shape of baseball gloves or shapeless armchairs made of sprayed polyurethane, they were embraced by the curators as sincere attempts to reposition the modern ideal in a different cultural landscape, in which the relationship between form and function was no longer univocal. Since the advent of the computer, formal experimentation and manufacturing have become easier, but the relationship between function and form has become even more complex. Nevertheless, curators have incorporated this change into their work as yet another set of conditions, and today can detect a modern attitude in the way contemporary designers consider their ideas in relation to the means at their disposal. Faith in empiricism, intuition, curiosity, and the ability to recognize mistakes have enabled the Museum's curators to keep the modern ideal

conversant with the design of their time.

Honesty, truth, and beauty, as ingredients of modernity, have been disseminated by the Museum via traveling shows, seminars, competitions, intellectual pressure on retailers and manufacturers, and publications. The ideals of beauty have evolved in the nearly seventy-five years since the inception of the collection, and the machine has evolved to attain capabilities once unthinkable. Yet, in the equation that results in modern, pure aesthetics may have become a variable, but the ethical aspects have remained constant.

Curators and the Collection

Curators are, literally, custodians of collections, guardians of the authenticity and quality of objects in their care. This description, while certainly appropriate for museums devoted to the preservation of the past, does not really apply to museums like The Museum of Modern Art, which write their own histories and are custodians of the present. The activity of a contemporary design curator is not based on the retrieval of existing proofs of pre-established generating rules but, rather, on the progressive detailing of new concepts in continuous evolution, requiring continuous shifts in perspective, from the particular to the general, from description to synthesis. The Museum's design collection has had all kinds of curators, from the caretaker to the hunter, from the historian to the

reporter, and is indeed a unique collection of their ideas.

The collection was crafted over many decades; all of its curators have made different contributions and left enduring legacies. In reaching the common goal of the modern ideal, each curator has shown a different personality, perspective, and agenda. The collection, as a history of ideas, is deeply human, rich in idiosyncrasies and contradictions, and yet its unified character is stronger than all of its discrepancies. The curators, selected and hired as if by elective affinity with the Museum's mission, have acknowledged their power as connoisseurs and their opportunity to influence what society at large sees and how it lives.

First, there was Philip Johnson, who, with Alfred Barr, called upon Plato and St. Thomas Aquinas as his authoritative guardian angels in order to define the design ideals at the Museum, in the catalogue for *Machine Art*. For Johnson, these embodied an ideal that involved not only clear and perfect beauty but also the recognition of industry as an essential component of culture. Johnson has been a curatorial presence at the Museum since its inception, able to deal with the art of all times. Although he resigned in 1934 to go into politics, he returned in 1947, an architect, and directed a united architecture and design program for five years beginning in 1949. From the mid-1950s to the present, Johnson has been a trustee, committee member, generous donor, and occasional curator at the Museum. A postmodern thinker before the term was coined, and endowed with awesome intellectual agility, he frequently changed direction, readjusted his aim, and exercised his considerable influence, love of provocation, intellectual prowess, and disarming wit.

John McAndrew, an architect and teacher, was the curator of the Department of Architecture and Industrial Art from 1937 to 1940. His annual series of Useful Objects exhibitions featured well-designed items available in stores and was meant to encourage designers and help the public select objects for their personal use; the series also generated numerous acquisitions.[17] By bringing the Museum's influence to bear on the commercial world for the first time, he pioneered many future departmental activities and showed that the Museum's aesthetic ideals could actually be within everybody's reach. Nonetheless, aesthetics were not his priority, and he drew a clear distinction between the work of a fine artist and that of a designer, whose work, he wrote in 1940, should be characterized by "Suitability to purpose . . . Suitability to material . . . Suitability to process of manufacture . . . Aesthetic quality."[18] In 1938, along with the exhibition *Alvar Aalto: Architecture and Furniture,* McAndrew also cemented the institution's ties to the Bauhaus with a comprehensive exhibition designed by Herbert Bayer and accompanied by a catalogue edited by Bayer and Ise and Walter Gropius; on this occasion the first Bauhaus objects entered the collection.

The industrial designer Eliot Noyes, the director of the Department of Industrial Design from 1940 to 1942 and then again in 1945 and 1946, had worked with Bauhaus masters Walter Gropius and Marcel Breuer at Harvard in the 1930s. His most well-known contribution was the 1940 competition Organic Design in Home Furnishings, conceived by Edgar Kaufmann, Jr., and won by Charles Eames and Eero Saarinen with their experiments in bent plywood, exhibited at the Museum the following year, which went on to become design classics. Noyes invoked William Morris, Adolf Loos, and Lewis Mumford in addition to Plato and St. Thomas Aquinas, and he articulated the idea of organic design as a beneficial and deep integration of the machine within human life.[19]

By the time he became director of the Department of Industrial Design in 1946, Kaufmann had already been involved in the Museum for at least eight years, brought in as early as 1938 as a member of the Committee of Architecture and Industrial Art, and

was recognized for his previous work on the Useful Objects shows.[20] His ability with complex productions was first displayed in his organization of the International Competition for Low-Cost Furniture Design in 1948, in which he not only exhorted designers from all over the world to use technological advancements from the military for civilian purposes, but he also made sure that the winning entries would be engineered and manufactured.[21]

In 1949, when Johnson became the director of the renamed Department of Architecture and Design, Kaufmann retained enough autonomy to continue to develop his famous Good Design program, which ran from 1950 to 1955 and consisted of three exhibitions every year, two at Chicago's Merchandise Mart, and one at the Museum around Christmas. In each show, about 175 (but sometimes as many as 400) objects were selected among the thousands available for sale in the United States and given a seal of approval in the form of a Good Design orange, black, and white tag. Like the Useful Objects series, the Good Design

program intended to influence the market for design in the United States; but it differed from the earlier series in openly trying to influence the retailers as well as the customers. Good Design had looser selection criteria than Useful Objects, and Kaufmann preferred to count on the jurors' taste and on eye-appeal, an approach repudiated by Johnson.[22] A somewhat loose aesthetic measure left more room not only for the team members' differences, but also for the public's insecurities and aspirations. Less intimidating and absolute than those from Machine Art, more contextualized and intellectually usable than those from the Useful Objects series, a great number of Good Design selections nevertheless made their way into the collection.

In 1951, Arthur Drexler began his thirty-five-year-long career at the Museum as curator of architecture and design. In the catalogue accompanying his first exhibition, *Eight Automobiles,* he wrote: "Automobiles are hollow, rolling sculpture,"[23] a statement that left little doubt as to the design policy at the Museum for the ensuing three

Exhibition of prize-winning designs, *Organic Design in Home Furnishings*, 1941

Pinin Farina. Cisitalia 202 GT Car. 1947. Aluminum body, 49 × 13½ × 57⅞" (125 × 401 × 147 cm). The Museum of Modern Art, New York. Gift of the manufacturer

decades; design and art were one. Although no automobiles were acquired as a direct result of this show, such acquisitions did begin in 1972, and the Museum now has a collection of six models, among them Pinin Farina's Cisitalia (1947), first shown in *Eight Automobiles*. In 1954, Johnson again resigned, this time to become a full-time architect (as well as a trustee), and Drexler assumed his administrative responsibilities, becoming director of the Department of Architecture and Design in 1956. Drexler's tenure as director lasted thirty years, the longest in the department, and his impact on both architecture and design was considerable. As the department grew, he created positions for numerous specialists in design, such as Mildred Constantine, who had been brought to the Museum by d'Harnoncourt in 1948 as Associate Curator of Graphic Design, but whose expertise was abundant in other areas, such as textiles, and Greta Daniel, Associate Curator of Design and the gatekeeper of the collection. Drexler, without reneging on the department's beneficial brush with retail, brought its curatorial stance back to aesthetics.

Drexler promoted his own ideas as well as those of many of his collaborators; the entire department flourished and the design collection grew, resulting in exhibitions of corporate design, sports equipment, crafts,

packaging, and artists' interpretations of design objects, which also generated acquisitions for the collection; among them were, notably, *Olivetti: Design in Industry* (1952), *The Package* (1959), *Two Design Programs: The Braun Company, Germany, and The Chemex Corporation, USA* (1964), and *The Object Transformed* (1966). Deeply inspired by the arts and architecture of Japan, Drexler deflated the accusations of eurocentrism that had often been turned on the department and, in addition to mounting the exhibition *The Architecture of Japan* and writing its now classic catalogue, he saw that the department began to acquire objects of design from Japan and elsewhere. An open mind was definitely necessary in the 1960s, when modernist architecture's foundations were shaken everywhere. Drexler sponsored the book that led the postmodern revolution in architecture, *Complexity and Contradiction in Architecture* by Robert Venturi, but he remained uncommitted as to its philosophy.

Drexler was the first director of the department to allow his program the luxury of looking backward as well as forward, and he carefully examined the collection for lacunae. With Greta Daniel, he supervised the first major installation of the collection in the winter of 1958–59 and the publication *Twentieth Century Design from the Collection of The Museum of Modern Art.*

At that time, the design collection numbered 850 objects. In 1960, Mildred Constantine organized an exhibition on *Art Nouveau*, and in 1970, F. Lanier Graham mounted an entire show on one of that style's most accomplished practitioners, Hector Guimard.

Emilio Ambasz, hired by Drexler in 1971, gave a boost to contemporary design at the Museum. A brilliant Princeton graduate in architecture, Ambasz organized extravagant and well-conceived exhibitions, such as *Italy: the New Domestic Landscape* (1972) and *The Taxi Project: Realistic Solutions for Today* (1976). Etched into the consciousness of every design enthusiast was the spectacular installation of the 1972 show within tall kiosks in the Museum's sculpture garden; and the show provided the collection with a windfall of important pieces from the 1960s, when Italy was at the forefront of both technical and formal design innovation. Ambasz said of his role in contrast to that of other types of curators: "I am the curator-hunter . . . the one that has an idea, goes out and raises funds, brings about institutional protection, and makes it happen."[24]

After Ambasz resigned for a full-time design and architecture career, Drexler hired historian J. Stewart Johnson, who was responsible for retrospective exhibitions on furniture designs by Isamu Noguchi (1978), Eileen Gray (1980), Marcel Breuer (1981), and Alvar Aalto (1984). Cara McCarty, who joined the Museum in 1984, took up the focus on contemporary design. After Drexler died in

Exhibition, *Good Design*, 1952

17

Installation, *Twentieth Century Design from the Collection of The Museum of Modern Art*, 1958–59

1987, the department was headed by architect Stuart Wrede, who had been brought in as the guest curator of an exhibition on the Swedish architect Gunnar Asplund in 1978 and who mounted many exhibitions in hitherto neglected areas of modern architecture and design, as well as a major show on the department's poster collection. During Wrede's tenure, McCarty's most important exhibitions, *Mario Bellini: Designer* in 1987 (on Bellini's groundbreaking work on electronic equipment and furniture), *Designs for Independent Living* in 1988 (on products for the aging and the physically disabled), *Information Art: Diagramming Microchips* in 1990 (a display of thirty-one computer-generated drawings of twenty-two circuits, along with actual computer chips), and *Modern Masks and Helmets* (1991) not only enriched the collection, but also presented an innovative interpretation of its formative principles. McCarty's interest in contemporary Japanese textiles, moreover, led to the formation of a fine collection that was subsequently perfected by Matilda McQuaid, who joined the department in 1987. Her diverse interests ranged from historical architecture and design to contemporary

engineering and textiles. Her previous academic work on women designers informed and strengthened some of her choices of exhibitions, such as the retrospective *Gunta Stölzl and Anni Albers* of 1990, or the first exhibition (1996) of work by the German architect and designer Lilly Reich, who was one of the most influential women practic-

ing in her field during the 1920s and 1930s. After McCarty had moved on to the Saint Louis Art Museum, the two curators organized *Structure and Surface: Contemporary Japanese Textiles*, with an installation designed by the architect Toshiko Mori (1998–99). During this period, Christopher Mount also organized several design exhibitions related to the collection, among them *Kaj Franck: Designer* (1992), *Designed for Speed: Three Automobiles by Ferrari* (1994), and *Refining the Sports Car: Jaguar's E-Type* (1996).

Architect Terence Riley became Chief Curator of Architecture and Design in 1992, at a time when modernism was out of vogue, after having been the director of the Arthur Ross Architecture Galleries at Columbia University, where he organized an exhibition that re-examined the Museum's 1932 Johnson and Hitchcock exhibition: *Modern Architecture—International Exhibition*. Riley has pursued parallel paths, for historical as well as contemporary issues, in the department, and organized important, well-received mid-size exhibitions on contemporary architects who have synthesized postmodernist thought into a new vision of the

Exhibition, *Italy: The New Domestic Landscape*, 1972

18

Exhibition, *Mario Bellini: Designer*, 1987

modern, among them Bernard Tschumi and Rem Koolhaas. He also added to the curatorial staff a mix of hunters, historians, reporters, and caretakers. Architectural historian Peter Reed joined the department in 1992 to work with Riley on the Frank Lloyd Wright retrospective, and this author joined the team in 1994 with a mandate to define the modern ideal in contemporary design. To date, this team has produced a series of major historical retrospectives and daring previews of new work encompassing both architecture and design: *Frank Lloyd Wright: Architect* (1994), *Mutant Materials in Contemporary Design* (1995), *Thresholds: Contemporary Design from the Netherlands* (1996), *Alvar Aalto: Between Humanism and Materialism* (1998), *Achille Castiglioni: Design!* (1998); *Different Roads: Automobiles for the Next Century* (1999), *Fernando and Humberto Campana and Ingo Maurer* (1999); *Mies in Berlin* (2001); and *Workspheres* (2001). Many of these and other exhibitions led to important acquisitions.

Acquisitions

Modern design recognizes certain characteristics that relate to both the form and the meaning of an object, the way it has been manufactured, the intentions of the designer and the manufacturer, and its impact on the world. There have been various formulations of the criteria according to which objects are deemed worthy of the Museum's collection, and the process of acquisition involves complex issues, such as funding, and collaboration among a select and knowledgeable group. Criteria may vary, but all concerned within the sphere of the collection agree on the basic principles. A 1984 statement by Drexler touches upon the core of this understanding: "An object is chosen for its quality because it is thought to achieve, or have originated, those formal ideals of beauty that have become the major stylistic concepts of our time. Significance is a more flexible criterion. It applies to objects that may not be entirely satisfactory for aesthetic or practical reasons but nevertheless have contributed importantly to the development of design."[25]

The collection is thus augmented by induction rather than deduction, and new acquisitions are discussed openly. Designers are not represented by entire bodies of work but, rather, by their most suitable pieces. The focus is on the objects themselves. The curators receive submissions from all over the world, conduct research on new and old objects, visit designers and schools, and actively seek the objects on a dedicated wish list, built over the years and including objects from all periods, from a Christopher Dresser bowl to a state-of-the-art racing

Exhibition, *Mutant Materials in Contemporary Design*, 1995

Exhibition, *Achille Castiglioni: Design!*, 1998

scull. Temporary exhibitions, as has been indicated, are a rich source of acquisitions. The curators meet several times a month to review the proposals, including unsolicited submissions, discuss them, and filter them into something of an ideal compilation. Twice a year, the curators present the objects that they would like to acquire to a Committee on Architecture and Design, composed of experts in design and architecture, some of them trustees, who vote to assign the final approval.

The Museum has been able to count on the generosity of an army of donors, manufacturers, retailers, designers, and collectors who have donated items to the collection. When it comes to contemporary design, manufacturers are often eager to provide the objects as gifts, upon request from the curators. In some cases, especially when it comes to historical items that are found in auctions or for sale in galleries, or items produced by young designers without the backing of a solid manufacturer, funds are provided by the Committee, by a number of support groups at the Museum, or sought from individuals devoted to a particular period, designer, country, or object.

Even though there is no fixed recipe

for successful inclusion, some principles of exclusion have, instead, become established traditions. A few of them are firm: no weapons, for instance, and no fashion items per se are permitted to enter the collection, albeit for different motives. In the case of weapons, we have this explanation by Drexler: "Deadly weapons are among the most fascinating and well-designed artifacts of our time, but their beauty can be cherished only by those for whom aesthetic pleasure is divorced from the value of life—a mode of perception the arts are not meant to encourage."[26] In the case of fashion, its perceived ephemerality positioned it decades ago outside the boundaries of the mission of the department (although guest curator Bernard Rudofsky organized a famous iconoclastic show, *Are Clothes Modern?* in 1944). Nonetheless, the department acquires textiles, some historical—by Anni Albers and Gunta Stölzl, for instance—some technical—such as erosion control mats and filters—and some designed for fashion applications, including an extensive collection of Japanese textiles. In 1987, a Mariano Fortuny y Madrazo gown was acquired, based upon a wish expressed by Drexler. It is one of only two garments in the collection, if a wetsuit is classified as a garment.

Some observers have attributed the ephemerality rule to so-called postmodernist style, and the collection has famously declined to include objects by the Italian Memphis group and other icons of the period. This choice seems more dictated by aesthetic criteria, rather than by ethical ones, much like Johnson's exclusion of Art Deco in his *Objects: 1900 and Today* show. In fact, there are numerous postmodern objects in the collection, for instance, Shiro Kuramata's furniture, which renders subtle and beautiful comments on the rigor of modernism.

The collection's relationship to the decorative arts and the crafts, whose production of one-off pieces made by hand is at

odds with the notion of serial industrial production, has been uneven and variegated. Although no question was ever raised when it came to modern masterpieces which, although not directly machine-made, were certainly inspired by the machine and intended to advance modern ideals, such as de Stijl or Bauhaus objects, various curators have at different times turned a curious gaze to the crafts and the decorative arts, as if to better define and delineate their own mission. Several idiosyncratic acquisitions, for instance wood bowls by James Prestini, who was briefly a part of the curatorial staff, may appear inconsistent with the rest of the collection, or others, like Mary Ann Toots Zinsky's work with glass, present interesting innovations in the use of materials. Moreover, even in the case of real industrial products, some advanced materials actually demand manual intervention, while some low-tech materials merely demand a crafts approach because of their essential

Mariano Fortuny y Madrazo. Delphos Tea Gown with Belt. 1907. Silk and glass beads, gown: 60½ × 19" (153.7 × 48.3 cm). The Museum of Modern Art, New York. Gift of Mrs. Susan G. Rossbach

Exhibition, *Structure and Surface: Contemporary Japanese Textiles*, 1998–99

nature. Experimentation, be it high-tech or low-tech, requires a hands-on approach, and the flexibility and novelty of the materials and manufacturing methods available today have stimulated the exploration of numerous possibilities.

De-accessions are rare and usually done in the interest of furthering the collection as a whole. In some cases, objects are de-accessioned and the funds from their sale used to acquire new objects from the same period. In others, designs just cannot seem to be able to stand the test of time. In 2001, for instance, a few objects made of plastics, acquired in 1944, 1956, and 1969, were de-accessioned because their material was in advanced state of deterioration. When it comes to modern objects, there can be an unknown and unpredictable lifespan of certain modern materials. One of the biggest problems to date is self-skinning polyurethane foam, in great vogue in the 1960s, whose surface hardens and cracks and whose body disintegrates with each passing year. The recent acquisition of objects made of biodegradable materials presents a new challenge for future curators and conservators.

Design in Our Time

Design today has to deal with its own set of priorities and responsibilities, such as a concern for the environment, a newly formulated responsibility toward other human beings, new technical advancements in manufacturing and distribution, a new sense of privacy and ownership of things and spaces, the immateriality of new forms of design, the interactivity that many objects allow, and the resurgence of local cultures in response to the global market, to name just a few. Yet, all design goes back to the same economy of goals and means. As new types of design and new issues present themselves, they are incorporated into the work of curators. Pedestals, platforms, walls, and wall texts—in other words, the way design is communicated and explained—are the elements that have changed the most, to match the public's changed requirements and accommodate new types of objects, from interfaces to computers and robots. But curators' expectations, as deftly expressed by Ambasz, remain the same, a desire to, "number one, present the phenomenon, two, invite interpretation . . . and see what meanings it has for the culture. [A museum] has to operate on a very reduced level . . . dealing . . . with complex problems and assuming responsibility [as] a monitoring institution, an evaluatory institution, certainly not . . . prescriptive."[27]

Thus, the curators are still scouting the world in search of emerging elements that can foster the modern ideal. The body of the collection and its intellectual history provide a solid reference, even though some of its mandates have ceased to be current. The machine, for instance, is not an efficient paradigm any more, as the profession of design, its creative process, and the way objects are used and understood today follow more organic and nonlinear behaviors. Similarly, as stated before, platonic beauty now seems just an ancient reference that has ceased to have currency.

The position of design, and the necessity to establish its importance and influence, is the spark that is able to motivate curators' enthusiasm. To this day, the public perception of design is frayed with ambiguity, mistaken by some as decoration, by others as engineering, and overall often underestimated in its preeminence as an intellectual model with the potential to reach far beyond the realm of commerce and art deep into the social fabric and material culture. The Museum's curators' ambitions, pursued with the same inductive theory as that established by their forebears, is to contribute to the construction of a modern ideal in continuous evolution.

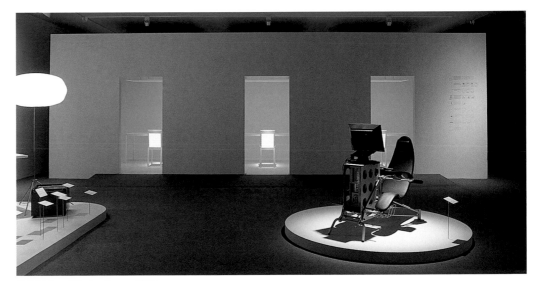

Exhibition, *Workspheres*, 2001

Notes

1. Provisional Charter granted to The Museum of Modern Art, September 19, 1929, by the New York State Board of Regents. Reprinted in Alfred H. Barr, Jr., "Chronicle of the Collection," in idem, *Painting and Sculpture in The Museum of Modern Art, 1929–1967*. (New York: The Museum of Modern Art, 1977): 620.
2. Nelson A. Rockefeller, letters to Philip Johnson, December 30, 1932, and January 13, 1933. Exhibition Files, Department of Registration, The Museum of Modern Art: exh. # 23.
3. See Philip Johnson, *Machine Art* (New York: The Museum of Modern Art, 1934). Reissued 1969, 1994.
4. N. Maffei, "John Cotton Dana and the Politics of Exhibiting Industrial Arts in the U.S., 1909–1929," *Journal of Design History*, vol. 13, no. 4 (2000): 301–318. As director of the Newark Museum in New Jersey, Dana pioneered the exhibition of mass-produced goods. He saw his museum's activities as a progressive response to the problems of increasing industrialization, an expanding consumer culture, and a search for a national aesthetic based on the machine. Dana hoped to reform the museum community, society, and industry. The first display of modern industrial design in America was a 1912 exhibition on the Deutscher Werkbund.
5. The Museum's first painting, Edward Hopper's *House by the Railroad* (1925), was acquired in 1930. In 1934 The Lillie P. Bliss collection, comprising masterpieces by Paul Cézanne, Paul Gauguin, Amedeo Modigliani, Georges Seurat, and Camille Pissarro, was acquired. In the same year, the first acquisitions in design, more than one hundred industrial objects, were chosen from the *Machine Art* exhibition.
6. Philip Johnson, letter to Alfred Barr, August 1931. Quoted in Terence Riley. *The International Style: Exhibition 15 and The Museum of Modern Art* (New York: Rizzoli and Columbia Books, 1992: 50.
7. "Introduction," *The Museum of Modern Art, New York: The History and the Collection* (New York: The Museum of Modern Art, 1984): 11.
8. Walter Gropius, "The Theory and Organization of the Bauhaus" (1923), in Herbert Bayer, Walter Gropius, and Ise Gropius, eds., *Bauhaus 1919–1928* (New York: The Museum of Modern Art, 1938): 22.
9. Barr, "Chronicle of the Collection": 620.
10. Ibid.
11. Philip Johnson, *Objects: 1900 and Today* (New York: The Museum of Modern Art, 1933): 6–7.
12. See Terence Riley, "Portrait of the Curator as a Young Man," in *Philip Johnson and The Museum of Modern Art*. Studies in Modern Art 6 (New York: The Museum of Modern Art, 1998): 34–69.
13. Serge Chermayeff and René d'Harnoncourt, "Design for Use," in *Art in Progress* (New York: The Museum of Modern Art, 1944): 194.
14. Edgar Kaufmann, Jr., *The Museum of Modern Art Department of Industrial Design*. The Museum of Modern Art Bulletin, vol. 14, no. 1 (fall 1946): 5.
15. Chermayeff and d'Harnoncourt, "Design for Use": 194.
16. Kaufmann, *Department of Industrial Design*: 3.
17. The series continued until 1948, and adapted to changing political conditions. In 1941–42, it was called *Useful Objects in Wartime under $10* and, in 1947, under Philip Johnson, it was named *100 Useful Objects of Fine Design (Available under $100).*
18. John McAndrew, *Useful Objects under Ten Dollars*. The Bulletin of The Museum of Modern Art, vol. 6, no. 6 (January 1940): 5–6.
19. Noyes used the following quotes: "Have nothing in your house that you do not know to be useful or believe to be beautiful," William Morris, 1860; "To find beauty in form instead of making it depend on ornament is the goal towards which humanity is aspiring," Adolf Loos, *Ins Leere Gesprochen*, 1898; and "Our capacity to go beyond the machine rests in our power to assimilate the machine. Until we have absorbed the lessons of objectivity, impersonality, neutrality, the lessons of the mechanical realm, we cannot go further in our development toward the more richly organic, the more profoundly human … the economic … and finally the integration of these principles in a new conception of the organic—these are the marks, already discernible, of our assimilation of the machine not merely as an instrument of practical action but as a valuable mode of life," Lewis Mumford, *Technics and Civilization*, 1934. Subsequently, Noyes worked for the industrial designer Norman Bel Geddes and then joined IBM, where he initiated a corporate program of design along the lines of the Olivetti Program.
20. According to the minutes of a meeting of the Museum's Committee on Architecture and Industrial Design in 1938, Philip L. Goodwin suggested the addition of a new member, Edgar Kaufmann, Jr., as one "who did a large part of the work of assembling the Museum's recent exhibition, *Useful Objects under Five Dollars."* The Museum of Modern Art Archives, Committee on Architecture and Industrial Art, minutes: December 7, 1938. For an extensive study of Kaufmann's role at the Museum and of his Good Design series, see Terence Riley and Edward Eigen, "Between the Museum and the Marketplace: Selling Good Design," in *The Museum of Modern Art at Mid-Century: At Home and Abroad*. Studies in Modern Art 4 (New York: The Museum of Modern Art, 1994): 150–179.
21. This competition focused on storage and seating that could be "integrated to the needs of modern living, production, and merchandizing." International Competition for Low-Cost Furniture Design (brochure and entry form), The Museum of Modern Art and the Museum Design Project, Inc., October 1948. Department of Architecture and Design, Archives.
22. The goals of the program were the following: "1. Greater consumer interest is to be focused on original design by taking advantage of its inherent news value. 2. To provide greater impetus for designers to produce good new products. 3. To encourage manufacturers to produce good design, and to draw their attention to the growing market by the wider consumer demand." This, of course, is quite different from a typical declaration of intent by Johnson.
23. Arthur Drexler, *8 Automobiles* (New York: The Museum of Modern Art, 1951): foreword.
24. Emilio Ambasz, interview by Sharon Zane, December 1993–January 1994. The Museum of Modern Art Oral History Project: 51.
25. Arthur Drexler, "Architecture and Design," in *The Museum of Modern Art, New York:* 385.
26. Ibid.: 388.
27. Ambasz, interview: 109–110.

Note to the Plates

The objects selected for this catalogue are highlights from The Museum of Modern Art's collection of design objects. They are arranged and discussed in nine thematic groupings, which delineate the history of modern design, as collected by the Museum for seventy-five years. These groupings provide a convenient way to consider a diverse collection, and are not fixed categories; in fact, some objects might easily have been included in more than one category.

Each illustrated work is accompanied by a caption, and occasionally also by a descriptive text. In the captions, the name of the designer (individual, group, or corporate) is followed by the name of the object and then its design date. The medium and dimensions follow, the latter in feet, inches, and centimeters, height before width before depth. The name of the manufacturer is given if it has not appeared as the designer. The date of manufacture follows in parentheses if it differs from the date of design. All of the objects are in the collection of The Museum of Modern Art; the means of acquisition conclude each caption.

The nine thematic sections are introduced by individual texts, signed by their authors. The texts for individual objects are signed with initials; the writers are Paola Antonelli, Bevin Cline, Tina di Carlo, Christian Larsen, Luisa Lorch, Matilda McQuaid, Christopher Mount, Peter Reed, and Terence Riley.

The nationalities and dates of the designers are given in the index at the end of this volume.

In the late nineteenth century, the unprecedented changes brought about by industrialization led designers and architects in the United States and Europe to turn from the past and reject historicism. Many committed themselves to developing aesthetic expressions appropriate for modern life, and their various tenets have formed the building blocks of the Museum's collection of design objects. The belief that art should be available to all regardless of class, and that it should reflect the industrial environment, embrace mass production, and articulate structure and materials had emerged by the turn of the century. Excessive ornamentation was eschewed, and an interest in the reduction of nature's organic forms into basic geometry was nurtured. Social principles, industrial mass production, and aesthetic abstraction marked important turning points for design, from the past into the modern.

Otto Wagner, a founder of the Vienna Secession, a group of artists who banded together against the establishment in 1898, believed: "The sole departure for our artistic work must be modern life." In industrial Scotland, Charles Rennie Mackintosh, the most prominent figure of the Glasgow School, urged artists to use, "in grace and beauty, the new forms and conditions that modern developments of life—social, commercial, and religious—insist upon." In the Netherlands, Gerrit Rietveld and the artists of de Stijl aimed to end the chaos brought about by World War I. They hoped that their radical Purist aesthetic would bring harmony between art and life to Europe.

Among designers of this period who advocated industrialization, Christopher Dresser is lauded as one of Europe's first full-fledged industrial designers. Viewing craftsmanship as outdated, he saw machine production as the basis of an entirely new lifestyle. His Toast Rack, for example, stressed simplicity, restrained ornamentation, and repeated motifs, all characteristics that facilitated mass production and wide distribution at low cost. Richard Riemerschmid, one of the organizers of the German Applied Art Secession of the end of the nineteenth century, promoted the idea of "products of the new arts and crafts . . . at a reasonable price," thus making manufactured design objects more available to all. Similarly, mass production was invoked in 1900 by Gustav Stickley, founder of the United Crafts Workshop (later the Craftsman Workshops) in Eastwood, New York, to make furniture in series; he believed that "certain purely mechanical processes . . . can be accomplished much better and more economically by machinery." Frank Lloyd Wright as well, in 1901, regarded the machine as "the only future of Art and Craft." In addition to designers, many manufacturers augmented the impact of industrialization on aesthetics. Chief among these were the Austrian companies Gebrüder Thonet and J. & J. Kohn. Their simple, well-designed, and relatively inexpensive bentwood furniture quickly found its way into Vienna's homes and cafés as well as to an international market. The Arts and Crafts concept of truth to materials, the use of materials in ways that interpret and complement their natural character, whether machine made or handcrafted, is seen in such pieces as a rectilinear oak and rush Settee by Stickley, a molded and curved Silver Loop-Handled Dish by Charles Robert Ashbee, and the ingenious steam-molded bentwood furniture of Thonet and Kohn.

The reduction of ornament and the paring down of design, resulting in clean surfaces that accentuate or complement their materials with rigorous simplicity, are seen in works by the designers of the Wiener Werkstätte (Viennese Workshop), a collaborative founded in 1903 by Josef Hoffmann and Koloman Moser that espoused many of the English Arts and Crafts movement's tenets of good design and high-quality craftsmanship. De Stijl relied on primary colors, and black and white. Mackintosh preferred flat planes of color, and wood painted white or ebonized, as in his Tea Table. Frequently, there is only the clear pattern of the wood grain itself; Rietveld's de Stijl furniture, accordingly, has very little or no upholstery, revealing simple construction with even the joints visible and at times accentuated, like the rivets incorporated in Dresser's earliest designs. Although trained as a botanist, Dresser abstracted and stylized nature to such an extreme that organic forms became geometric. There is also a rectilinear quality to the nature-inspired designs of Mackintosh, and indeed much of his later work is strictly geometric. In the same vein, Wright's Side Chair deliberately avoids curves; the horizontals, verticals, and planar qualities of the piece are emphasized. The canted backrest extends from the rear stretcher below the seat to the crest rail, generating a strong planar dimension.

The Wiener Werkstätte, which popularized the Secession style in furniture, metalwork, graphics, bookbinding, textiles, and glass, also favored repetitive geometric patterns. The simple rhythmic cadence of squares on Hoffmann's Fruit Bowl and Otto Prutscher's Compote Dish underlies their reductive order. Hoffmann's Liqueur Glasses are smooth geometric shapes devoid of ornament, essentially triangles supporting half circles. In the furniture of Rietveld, there are only straight lines and right angles. His Hanging Lamp, made of electrical wiring and three incandescent bulbs, is composed of horizontals and verticals, parallels and perpendiculars, which do not touch, suggesting infinite continuity while emulating the precision of machine products. His Red Blue Chair exemplifies de Stijl rigor in art and design.

Modernism was a new aesthetic embracing sweeping, universal change. No turn-of-the-century designer embodied all of its fundamental premises; however, collectively the principles put forth by their impassioned search for a new aesthetic provide the basis for the modern era in design.

—Bevin Cline

Gebrüder Thonet's bentwood Vienna Café Chair was for many years considered Vienna's official café chair. It was simple and attractive, and made from six parts that required minimum joinery and were easily assembled on location. The chair was inexpensive, durable, lightweight, and available in a variety of seat designs and stretcher configurations. It embodied all the reasons for Thonet's great success.

Michael Thonet, originally a cabinetmaker and the founder of Gebrüder Thonet in 1853, perfected a process of steaming wood rods and placing them in metal molds to dry. A number of standardized sections of bent beech wood were then joined with ordinary hardware rather than the intricate hand-carved joints of conventional furniture making. Although this was not the first bentwood chair, Thonet's revolutionary mass-production technique simplified and shortened the expensive labor-intensive process needed to produce it. He was able to manipulate rods into an infinite variety of curvilinear shapes, creating effects of lightness and transparency. Simple pieces, such as the Café Chair, were well suited for commercial use in restaurants, hotels, and assembly halls. A wide range of items, including not just chairs but tables, settees, and rocking sofas, among others, was sold internationally by Gebrüder Thonet branch offices and through catalogues in several languages. This model was the second least expensive item in the catalogue and eventually became one of Thonet's best-selling models, widely copied by his competitors. Supplying durable, attractive designs at affordable prices to diverse clients, Gebrüder Thonet served as a model for early twentieth-century designers and manufacturers. The Vienna Café Chair is still in production, and is used and recognized worldwide. —B.C.

Gebrüder Thonet
Vienna Café Chair (no. 18). 1876
Beech wood, 33⅜ × 17 × 20⅛"
(84.8 × 43.2 × 51.1 cm). Purchase Fund

William Morris
Chrysanthemum Pattern Printed
Fabric (no. 23612). 1884
Cotton, 37 × 37¾" (94 × 95.9 cm).
Manufacturer: J. H. Thorp & Co., Inc.,
USA (c. 1942). Gift of Edgar
Kaufmann, Jr.

Reacting against the precipitous industrialization of nineteenth-century Britain, William Morris condemned industry and advocated a return to traditional hand labor and craftsmanship. Contrary to many forward-looking designers of his time, but in perfect step with his mentor John Ruskin, the most prominent aesthete of the day, he believed the machine incapable of producing true art and that the production of art through handicraft was the basis of a proper society. A founder of the English Arts and Crafts movement and an advocate of English socialism, Morris wished to create well-designed, well-made products for the masses and to teach them how to use their own handicraft skills to make a living. He advocated an "art of the people, by the people, and for the people," through which the satisfying and financially rewarding production of handcrafted objects would improve the lives of the lower classes.

The inherent paradox of this point of view was that handwork was not as efficient as machine production and, therefore, its products tended to be costly. Contrary to Morris's well-intentioned principles, the elaborate processes required for the products produced by Morris & Co. made his design objects and woven textiles available for the most part only to the wealthy. For example, the large complicated pattern of the Chrysanthemum Pattern Printed Fabric was available in a number of different colors in cotton or linen. But it required thirty-four blocks for printing and was, consequently, the most expensive of all of Morris's printed textiles. This version, with pale colors on a white background, is most likely a twentieth-century variant. —B.C.

Charles Rennie Mackintosh's design of the Side Chair for the Luncheon Room of Miss Catherine Cranston's Argyle Street Tearooms was the first in a series of high-backed chairs that were never intended for wide reproduction. Designed specifically for the tables in the center of the tearoom, it was one of the first commissions in which Mackintosh demonstrated his characteristic integration of furniture and architecture.

Oval slotted panels were fitted into the tall uprights of the chairs, which served no function other than as architectural elements, emphasizing the long narrow space in which they stood. By screening out the sides of the room, the exaggerated height and concave forms of the furniture carved out a private island in the middle of the tearoom. The chair shows not only Mackintosh's decorative use of structural elements and his love of bold, pure geometries but

also the way in which the extended two-dimensional form of the high back and oval element heightens the object's ability to delineate and contain space. The chair was first exhibited in an interior in Vienna, at the eighth exhibition of the Secessionist movement in 1900, where Mackintosh met the Viennese designer Josef Hoffmann, whose work in the years that followed showed the influence of the Scottish designer's geometric idiom.

Mackintosh trained at the Glasgow School of Art prior to the founding of an architectural curriculum there. He also served as an apprentice to the Glasgwegan architect John Hutchinson. Upon completing his studies in 1889, he was hired as a draftsman by the architectural firm of Honeyman and Keppie, where in 1896 his design won the competition for a new Glasgow School of Art, one of his most celebrated works. —T.d.C.

Charles Rennie Mackintosh
Side Chair. 1897
Oak and silk, 54⅜ × 20 × 18"
(138.1 × 50.8 × 45.7 cm). Gift of the
Glasgow School of Art

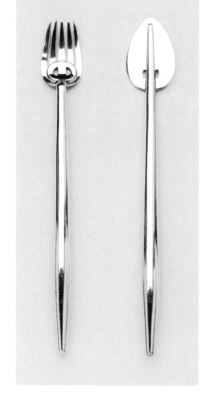

Charles Rennie Mackintosh
Fish Knife and Fork. 1900
Silver-plated nickel, knife: 9⅛ × 1¼"
(23.2 × 3.2 cm); fork: 8⅞ × 1⅛"
(22.5 × 2.9 cm). Gift of the University
of Glasgow

Charles Rennie Mackintosh
Tea Table. 1904
Ebonized wood, 24 × 36¾ × 19¾"
(61 × 93.3 × 50.2 cm). Guimard Fund

Christopher Dresser
Toast Rack. c. 1878
Electroplated silver, 5¼ × 5¼ × 4¼"
(13.3 × 13.3 × 10.8 cm). Manufacturer:
James Dixon & Sons, England.
Mrs. John D. Rockefeller 3rd
Purchase Fund

Christopher Dresser
Claret Pitcher. c. 1880
Glass, silver plate, and ebony, 16⅝ ×
5¼ × 4" (42.2 × 13.3 × 10.2 cm) diam. at
base. Manufacturer: Hukin & Heath,
England. Gift of Mrs. John D.
Rockefeller 3rd

The simple geometry of this elongated Claret Pitcher is characteristic of Christopher Dresser's designs, which stand in stark contrast to the heavily ornamented styles of his time. Dresser had studied Japanese decorative arts, which influenced his own designs and those of his more progressive contemporaries. In this pitcher, the long, vertical ebony handle is almost a direct quotation of the bamboo handles on Japanese vessels. As in many of his designs for metalwork, the fittings on the claret pitcher are made from electroplated metal, a technological innovation that made silverware available to a growing middle class before the turn of the century. The exposed rivets and joints presage the enthusiasm for the machine aesthetic in industrial design of several decades later.

A trained botanist as well as a designer, Dresser was strongly inspired by the underlying structures of natural forms and by his interest in technological progress. While he shared some of the theories of the English Arts and Crafts movement, which sought to replace the often-shoddy design of mass-produced goods with skilled handcraftsmanship, Dresser was completely committed to quality design for machine production, and is one of the world's first industrial designers. —L.L.

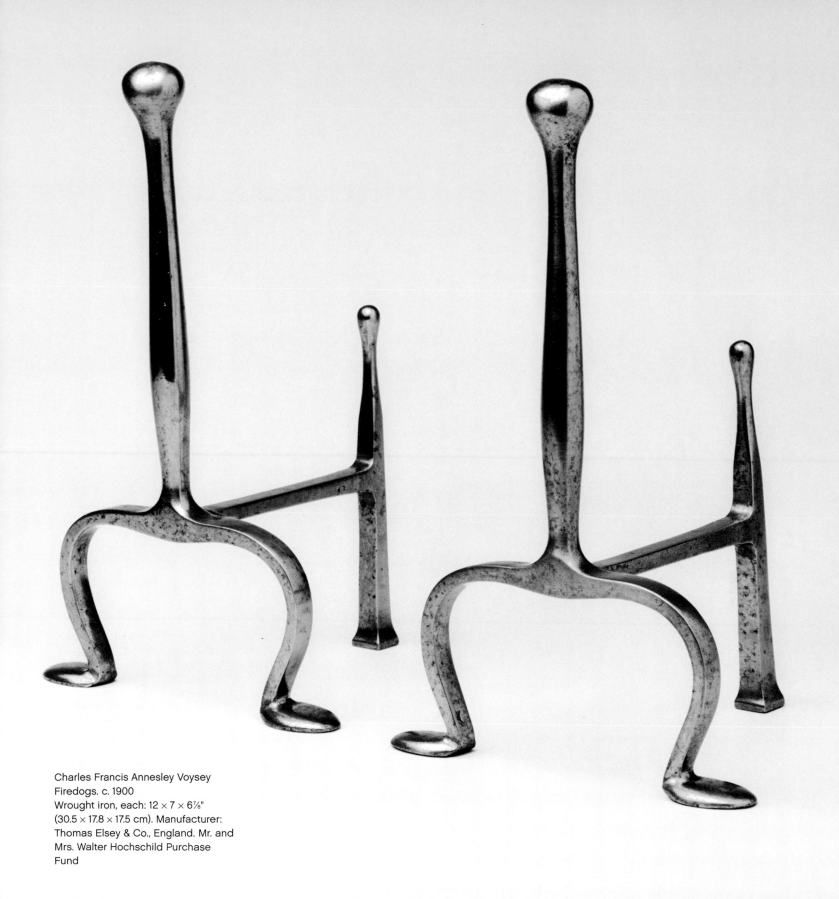

Charles Francis Annesley Voysey
Firedogs. c. 1900
Wrought iron, each: 12 × 7 × 6⅞"
(30.5 × 17.8 × 17.5 cm). Manufacturer:
Thomas Elsey & Co., England. Mr. and
Mrs. Walter Hochschild Purchase
Fund

Richard Riemerschmid
Mustard Pot. c. 1897
Glazed stoneware, 8 × 4½ × 5½"
(20.3 × 11.4 × 14 cm) diam.
Manufacturer: Reinhold Merkelbach,
Germany. Phyllis B. Lambert Fund

Richard Riemerschmid
Drapery Fabric. 1908
Printed cotton, 7¾ × 7¾"
(19.7 × 19.7 cm). Manufacturer:
Deutsche Werkstätten für
Handwerkskunst, Germany. Phyllis
B. Lambert Fund

Archibald Knox
Jewel Box. c. 1900
Silver, mother-of-pearl, turquoise,
and enamel, 4 × 11½ × 6½"
(10.2 × 29.2 × 16.5 cm). Manufacturer:
H. C. Craythorne and Liberty & Co.,
England. Gift of the family of Mrs.
John D. Rockefeller 3rd

Charles Robert Ashbee
Silver Loop-Handled Dish. 1901
Silver and lapis lazuli, 2¹¹⁄₁₆ × 7¹³⁄₁₆ × 4⅜"
(6.8 × 19.8 × 11.1 cm). Manufacturer:
Guild of Handicraft Ltd., England.
Estée and Joseph Lauder Design
Fund

Josef Hoffmann
Flatware. 1905
Silver-plate on nickel silver,
largest: 10½" (26.7 cm) long.
Manufacturer: Wiener
Werkstätte, Austria. Estée
and Joseph Lauder Design
Fund

Josef Hoffmann
Fruit Bowl. c. 1904
Painted metal, 3¾ × 8½" (9.5 ×
21.6 cm) diam. Manufacturer:
Franz Wittman KG, Austria (1974).
Philip Johnson Fund

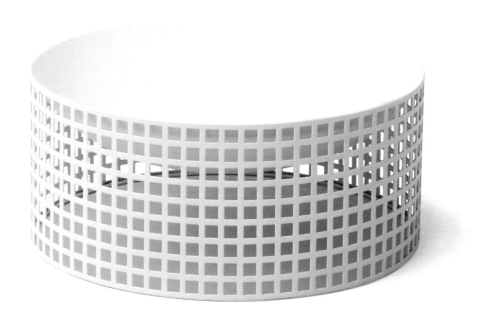

Josef Hoffmann
Sitzmaschine Chair with Adjustable
Back (model 670). c. 1905
Bent beech wood and sycamore
panels, 43½ × 28¼ × 32" (110.5 ×
71.8 × 81.3 cm). Manufacturer: J. & J.
Kohn, Austria. Gift of Jo Carole and
Ronald S. Lauder

Josef Hoffmann designed the
Sitzmaschine (machine for sitting)
for his Purkersdorf Sanatorium in
Vienna. The sanatorium, one of the
first important commissions given to
a member of the Wiener Werkstätte,
represents one of Hoffmann's earliest experiments in unifying a building and its furnishings as a total
work of art.

The Sitzmaschine Chair makes
clear reference to an adjustable-

back English Arts and Crafts chair
known as the Morris chair, designed
by Philip Webb around 1866. It also
stands as an allegorical celebration
of the machine. This armchair, with its
exposed structure, demonstrates a
rational simplification of forms suited
to machine production. Yet, at the
same time, the grid of squares pierc-
ing the rectangular back splat, the
bentwood loops that form the arm-
rests and legs, and the rows of

knobs on the adjustable back illustrate the fusion of decorative and
structural elements typical of the
Wiener Werkstätte style. J. & J. Kohn
produced and sold this chair in a
number of versions, most of which
had cushions on the seat and back,
until at least 1916. The Kohn firm produced many designs by Hoffmann, in
one of the first successful alliances
between a designer and industry in
Vienna. —L.L.

Otto Prutscher
Compote Dish. c. 1907
Flashed and cut glass, 8 × 5⅞"
(20.3 × 15 cm) diam. Manufacturer:
E. Bakalowits & Söhne, Austria. Estée
and Joseph Lauder Design Fund

Otto Wagner
Railing. 1899
Painted cast iron, 28¼ × 46½ × 3"
(71.8 × 118 × 7.6 cm). Dorothy Cullman
Purchase Fund

This cast-iron fragment comes from a quayside railing along the Danube canal in Vienna. It is largely undecorated, and has relatively minimal detailing. Otto Wagner achieved visual interest by juxtaposing vertical slats with geometrized wreathlike circular forms, which perhaps recall imperial decorations and trappings, and remind us that turn-of-the-century Vienna was the capital of the Austro-Hungarian Empire.

Wagner argued for simplicity and a new "realist" style, implying that modern designers should use modern materials and clear methods of construction. He gave shape to his ideas in many buildings and ambitious city-planning projects, which were designed in Vienna as the city expanded beyond its old medieval boundaries. His prolific output and progressive ideas influenced an entire generation, and firmly established him as one of the forefathers of a rational modern architecture. —P.R.

Josef Hoffmann
Liqueur Glasses. c. 1908
Blown glass, largest: 5¼ × 2¼"
(13.3 × 5.7 cm) diam.
Manufacturer: J. & L. Lobmeyr,
Austria. Joseph H. Heil Fund

Otto Wagner
Stool. 1904
Bentwood and aluminum,
18½ × 16 × 16" (47 × 40.6 × 40.6 cm).
Manufacturer: Gebrüder Thonet,
Austria. Estée and Joseph Lauder
Design Fund

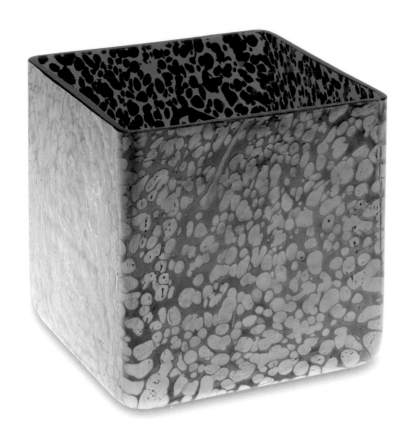

Koloman Moser
Vase. 1902
Glass, 6 × 6 × 6" (15.2 × 15.2 × 15.2 cm).
Manufacturer: Glasfabrik Johann
Loetz Witwe, Austria. Estée and
Joseph Lauder Design Fund

Daum Frères
Vase. c. 1900
Hand-painted sculpted glass,
8¼ × 3½ × 2¾" (21 × 8.9 × 7 cm).
Phyllis B. Lambert Fund

Gustav Stickley
Settee. 1905
Oak and rush, 49 × 48 × 24"
(124.5 × 121.9 × 61 cm). Manufacturer:
Craftsman Workshops, USA. Gift of
Susan de Menil, Edgar Smith, Beth
Cathers, and Nick Dembrosky

Frank Lloyd Wright
Office Armchair. 1904–06
Painted steel and oak, 36½ × 21 × 25"
(92.7 × 53.3 × 63 cm). Manufacturer:
Van Dorn Iron Works Co., USA.
Gift of Edgar Kaufmann, Jr.

Frank Lloyd Wright
Side Chair. 1904
Oak and leather, 35¾ × 15 × 18⅝"
(90.8 × 38.1 × 47.3 cm). Gift of the
designer

Frank Lloyd Wright's Side Chair demonstrates a startling simplification of parts, emphasizing the horizontal and vertical planes of the seat and back, uninterrupted by decorative carving. Allowing the canted backrest to span from the rear stretcher below the seat to above the crest rail (at shoulder height) gives a great spatial sense and planar dimension. The back seems to float free within the right angles of the chair's frame.

The clear structural expression and rational production as well as the deliberate avoidance of curved forms are indicative of the principles Wright espoused in a seminal talk, "The Art and Craft of the Machine," in 1901, where he stated his belief in machines that were suited to the repetition of simple linear motions. Inspired by the British Arts and Crafts movement, Wright also advocated reform, especially in the design of the American home for which he believed the machine could be an ally: "Now let us learn from the Machine. It teaches us that the beauty of wood lies first in its qualities as wood . . . that all wood carving is apt to be a forcing of the material, an insult to its finer possibilities as a material having in itself intrinsically artistic properties, of which its beautiful markings is one, its texture another, its color a third."

For Wright, furniture was an integral part of a building, and he conceived architectural spaces and their contents as total works of art. This chair was originally designed for the Larkin Building in Buffalo and was also used in his own homes in Oak Park, Illinois, and at Taliesin in Spring Green, Wisconsin. It is also an important precursor to one of the most famous of all twentieth-century designs—Gerrit Rietveld's Red Blue Chair. —P.R.

Gerrit Rietveld
Red Blue Chair. c. 1923
Painted wood, 34⅛ × 26 × 33"
(86.7 × 66 × 83.8 cm). Gift of
Philip Johnson

In the Red Blue Chair, Gerrit
Rietveld manipulated rectilinear vol-
umes and examined the interaction
of vertical and horizontal planes,
much as he did in his architecture.
Although the chair was originally
designed in 1918, its color scheme
of primary colors (red, yellow, blue)
plus black—so closely associated
with the de Stijl group and its most
famous theorist and practitioner Piet
Mondrian—was applied to it around
1923. Hoping that much of his furniture would eventually be mass-
produced rather than handcrafted,
Rietveld aimed for simplicity in construction. The pieces of wood that
comprise the Red Blue Chair are in
the standard lumber sizes readily
available at the time.

Rietveld believed there was a
greater goal for the furniture designer
than just physical comfort: the well-
being and comfort of the spirit. He
and his colleagues in the de Stijl art
and architecture movement sought to
create a utopia based on a harmonic
human-made order. —C.M.

Gerrit Rietveld
Hanging Lamp. 1920
Wood, glass, and tubular bulbs, 41 ×
15¾ × 15¾" (104.1 × 40 × 40 cm).
Manufacturer: G. A. Van de
Groenekan, the Netherlands (1982).
Emilio Ambasz Fund

Gerrit Rietveld
Table Lamp. 1925
Metal and half-painted glass bulb,
15 × 7¾ × 4½" (38.1 × 19.7 × 11.4 cm).
Gift of the designer

Gerrit Rietveld
Child's Wheelbarrow. 1923
Painted wood, 12½ × 11⅜ × 33½"
(31.8 × 28.9 × 85.1 cm). Manufacturer:
Gerard Van de Groenekan, the
Netherlands (1958). Gift of Jo Carole
and Ronald S. Lauder

2 | Machine Art

The Museum's *Machine Art* exhibition of 1934 presented over four hundred rigorously precise objects, such as propellers, coils, springs, ball bearings, and laboratory glass objects on pedestals, to be considered works of art, just as the abstract sculptures of Jean Arp and Constantin Brancusi were. The thrust of the exhibition was purely aesthetic, focusing on the unintentional beauty of the machine. According to the Museum's press release, the show's organizers, Alfred H. Barr, Jr., and Philip Johnson, selected objects that displayed "beauty—mathematical, mechanical, and utilitarian" and demonstrated a purity of form. The minimal aesthetic of these objects, designed solely with function in mind, resulted in unadorned forms, recalling ideal geometries that aspire to Plato's notion of beauty. Each object was pared down to its basic components. These objects were beautiful in part because they had function but most of all because they embodied the dynamic influence of the machine. While their functionality was acknowledged, the curators quoted from Plato (*Philebus*) in the catalogue: "By beauty of shape I do not mean, as most people would suppose, the beauty of living figures or of pictures, but, to make my point clear, I mean straight lines and circles, and shapes, plane or solid, made from them by lathe, ruler and square. These are not, like other things, beautiful relatively, but always and absolutely."

The curators' selections of industrially designed objects combined rhythm derived from the repetition of form with the sensuous surfaces of modern materials, such as porcelain, aluminum, and steel, and correct proportion. As such, they were seen as highly preferable to the prevailing *moderne*, streamline, or Art Deco styles. These, while also inspired by their generation's devotion to the machine, were ornamental styles, and much of the new thinking in art and architecture criticism was leading to a greater emphasis on abstraction, utility, and geometry.

A number of pieces of furniture in the show were produced by well-known contemporary architects and designers, such as Marcel Breuer, Le Corbusier, and Gilbert Rohde. However, most of the objects were created not by artists, architects, and designers, but by machinists. Not surprisingly, the controversial exhibition content garnered much attention in the press, both positive and negative, ranging from cartoons to philosophical essays.

Fascination with the beauty of the machine was widespread in the early years of the twentieth century, evident in the work of Francis Picabia, the French Purists Amédée Ozenfant and Fernand Léger, and Le Corbusier. In America, where the machine was exalted to cult status, the photographer Margaret Bourke-White captured a world for the cover of *Life* magazine where "dynamos were more beautiful than pearls"; Charles Demuth painted grain silos, likening them to temples radiant with light; and Charles Sheeler photographed the Ford Motor Company's River Rouge plant, declaring: "Our factories are substitutes for religious expression." In 1934, the aesthetic ideals of the *Machine Art* exhibition could be recognized in such acquisitions by the Museum as Charles Sheeler's painting of an industrial scene, *American Landscape* (1930), and the clean forms of Brancusi's unadorned, bronze sculpture *Bird in Space* (1928).

The principles of platonic beauty and the unintentional aesthetics of machine parts and industrial products have continued to inspire Museum acquisitions. Examples are the aluminum Cookie Cutting Wheel by an unknown designer, which echoes a turbine or machine gear, and the CSS/Winfield Unique Key Card, a simple stainless-steel rectangle with a pattern of perforations: a precise and elegant geometric design without embellishment. Nonetheless, notions of what constitutes beauty continue to evolve. Many recent acquisitions foster the idea that beauty resides within a multiplicity of possibilities, as opposed to one pure ideal of form. Thus, some objects designed early in the century were not acquired until much later, owing to the wider scope of criteria of the recent past as against that of the first years of the Museum. Édouard-Wilfred Buquet's 1927 Desk Lamp was acquired in 1977 and appeals to a machine aesthetic in its materials, nickel-plated brass and aluminum, but also to an interest in biomorphism, its skeletal parts pivoting much like the human shoulder, elbow, and wrist, and allowing for countless adjustments. A Hairdryer made by Müholos Ltd. between 1910 and 1930 and acquired in 1986, alludes not just to an arm but an entire body. The gleaming rounded forms of the Streamliner Meat Slicer, designed c. 1940 by Egmont Arens and Theodore C. Brookhart and acquired in 1989, call to mind an animal carcass. Mallory Industries' 1991 3-Dimensional Cams, acquired in 1992, are made of aluminum, a typically industrial material with a particularly lush finish. They are machine parts, designed by machines (computers) for machines, with curious and complex distorted surfaces.

Computer design, a method not imaginable in the 1930s, has resulted in a variety of inadvertently beautiful objects, which continue to be explored in various ways in the collection. In the Museum's 1990 *Information Art* exhibition, the paradigm of machine art shifted from an industrial mode to an electronic one, while the aesthetics became even more abstract. This exhibition explored the design of microelectronics with printed, enlarged, computer-generated plots of electronic pathways for integrated circuitry, mounted on the gallery walls. These arresting miniature electronic machines were not originally meant for the human eye; but they created compelling abstract works of art, once their various geometric forms were revealed. Seen as an electronic language and in the contemporary context of multiple levels of meaning, these works continue to expand our definition of beauty.

—Bevin Cline

Sven Wingquist
Self-Aligning Ball Bearing. 1907
Chrome-plated steel, 1¾ × 8½"
(4.4 × 21 .6 cm) diam. Manufacturer:
S.K.F. Industries, Inc., USA (1929). Gift
of the manufacturer

Both efficient and beautiful, the ball bearing can be seen as an emblem of the machine age—a name often used to define the 1920s and 1930s, when industrial designers as well as consumers took a new interest in the look and style of commercial products. Good design was considered by modernists as essential to the elevation of society, and in 1934, this ball bearing was among the first design works to enter The Museum of Modern Art's collection.

This sturdy steel ball bearing is composed of a double layer of balls in a race. This type of bearing was structurally superior to the sliding bearing, which wastes energy in realigning machinery shafts thrown off during assembly-line manufacturing. The self-aligning quality of the ball bearing made it a superior product, since the bearing could absorb some shaft misalignment without lowering its endurance. —P.A.

American Steel & Wire Co.
Bearing Spring. Before 1934
Steel, 2½ × 1⁵⁄₁₆" (6.4 × 3.4 cm) diam.
Gift of the manufacturer

Westinghouse Electric &
Manufacturing Co.
Ball and Socket Suspension Insulator.
Before 1931
Glazed porcelain and cast iron,
7 × 10" (17.8 × 25.4 cm) diam.
Gift of the manufacturer

Müholos Ltd.
Hairdryer. Before 1930.
Brass and metal, 56 × 20 × 25"
(142.2 × 50.8 × 63.5 cm).
Marshall Cogan Purchase Fund

Aluminum Company of America
Outboard Propeller. Before 1934
Aluminum, 24" (61 cm) diam. Gift of
the manufacturer

Henry Disston & Sons, Inc.
Cross-Cut Saw. Before 1934
Steel and wood, 36" (91.4 cm) diam.
Gift of the manufacturer

American Steel & Wire Co.
Textile Spring. Before 1934
Steel, 9¼ × 2¼" (23.5 × 5.7 cm).
Gift of the manufacturer

Browne & Sharpe Manufacturing Co.
Outside Firm-Joint Calipers.
Before 1934
Tempered steel, largest: 8½ ×
6½ × ½" (21.6 × 16.5 × 1.3 cm).
Gift of the manufacturer

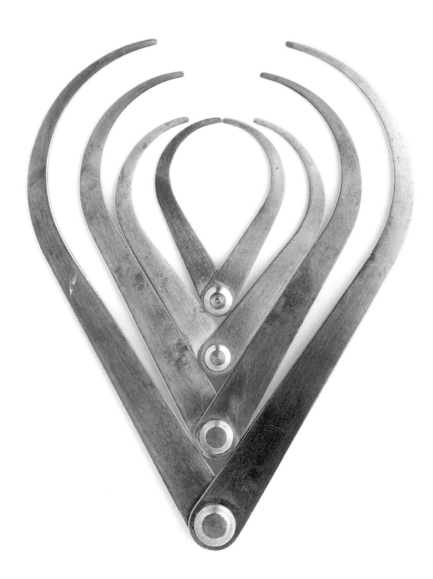

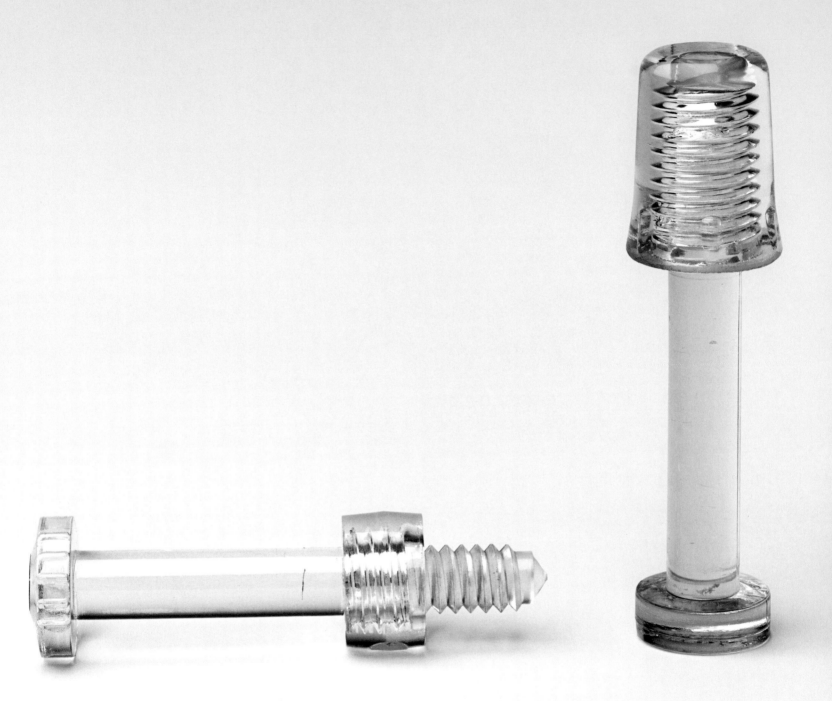

Corning Glass Works
Glass Nuts and Bolts. Before 1942
Borosilicate glass, largest: 6¼ × 1½"
(15.9 × 3.8 cm). Gift of the manufacturer

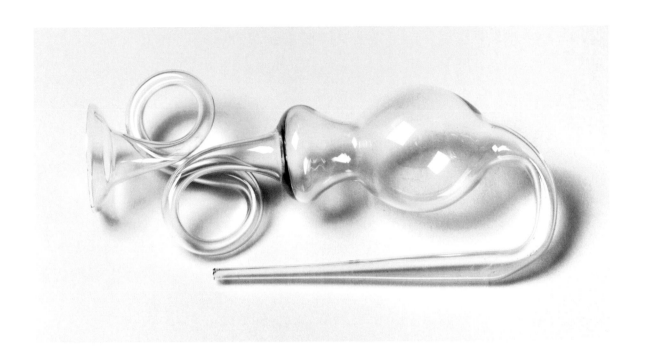

Designer unknown
Laboratory Glassware. n.d.
Borosilicate glass, 6 × 3 × 1½"
(15.2 × 7.6 × 3.8 cm).
Purchase

Coors Porcelain Co.
Evaporating Dish. Before 1946
Glazed porcelain, ⅞ × 4¼"
(2.2 × 10.8 cm) diam.
Purchase

Rosenthal Porzellan AG
Mold for Rubber Toy Balloon.
Before 1958
White porcelain, 9 × 2"
(22.9 × 5.1 cm) diam.
Gift of the manufacturer

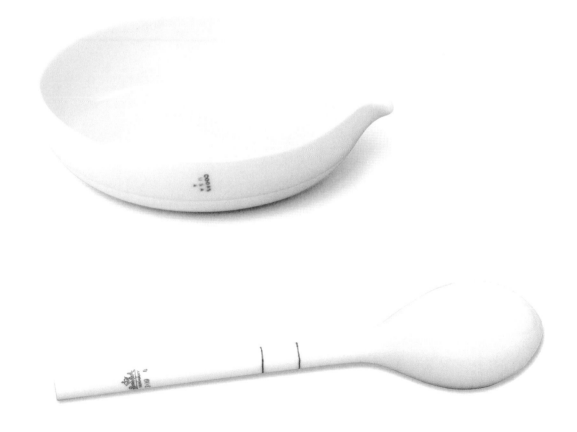

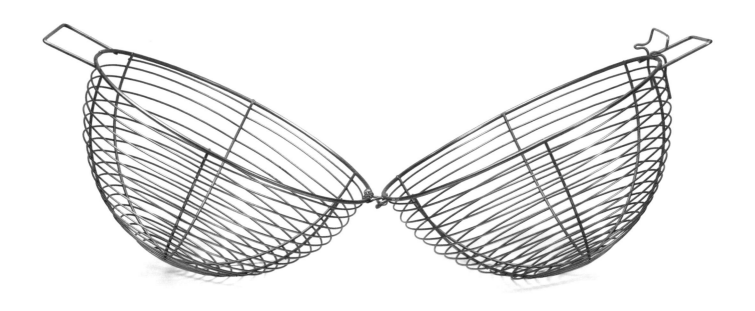

M. Schimmel
Salad Basket. c. 1946
Metal wire, 10" (25.4 cm) diam.
Manufacturer: Raymar Industries, Inc.,
USA (c. 1947). Purchase

Aluminum Cooking Utensil Co.
Wear-Ever Rotary Food Press. 1932
Aluminum, steel, and wood, 9 × 11⅜"
(22.9 × 28.9 cm) diam. Gift of Lewis &
Conger

Aluminum Cooking Utensil Co.
Wear-Ever Mixing Bowl. n.d.
Aluminum, 5 × 9⅛" (12.7 × 23.2 cm) diam.
Purchase

Vollrath Co.
Kitchen Scoop. Before 1956
Stainless steel, 13 × 5½"
(33 × 14 cm) diam. Purchase

Designer unknown
Measuring Spoon and Scale
(Ladle and Stand). n.d.
Cast aluminum, 3¼ × 13" (8.3 × 33 cm).
Manufacturer: French (c. 1953).
Gift of H. A. Mack & Co. Inc.

Édouard-Wilfred Buquet
Desk Lamp. 1927
Nickel-plated brass, aluminum, and
lacquered wood, 36 × 5⅛" (91.5 × 15 cm)
diam. at base. D. S. and R. H.
Gottesman Foundation

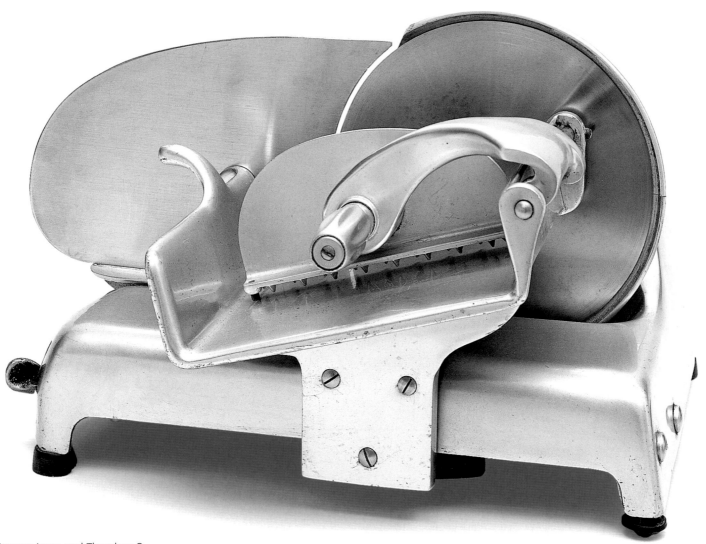

Egmont Arens and Theodore C.
Brookhart
Streamliner Meat Slicer (model 410).
c. 1940
Aluminum, steel, and rubber,
13 × 20¼ × 17" (33 × 51.4 × 43.2 cm).
Manufacturer: Hobart, USA (1945).
Gift of Eric Brill in memory of Abbie
Hoffman

Designer unknown
Cookie Cutting Wheel. 1953
Aluminum and plastic, 4 × 5"
(10.2 × 12.7 cm) diam. Manufacturer:
Foley Manufacturing Co., USA.
Department Purchase

Designer unknown
Cake Cutter. c. 1935
Steel and wire, 5¾ × 11⅜"
(14.6 × 28.9 cm) diam.
Manufacturer: American (c. 1940).
Gift of Bloomingdale Bros., Inc.

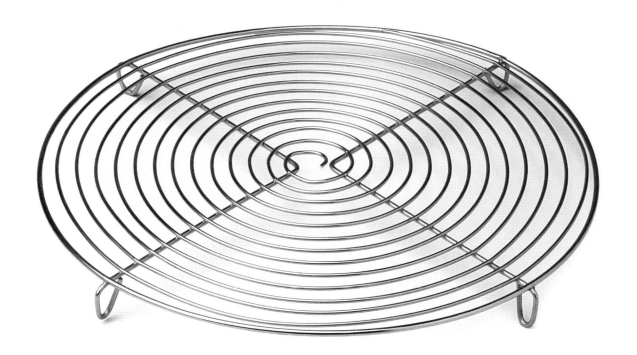

Designer unknown
Cake Cooler. 1950
Metal wire, ¾ × 10¾" (1.9 × 27.3 cm)
diam. Manufacturer: Phalanx
Stainless Steel Co., USA. Gift of Lewis
& Conger

Designer unknown
12-Cut Pie Marker. Before 1956
Cast aluminum, 2½ × 9⅝"
(6.4 × 24.4 cm) diam. Manufacturer:
Italian. Department Purchase

American Steel & Wire Co.
Door Closer Bracket. Before 1934
Steel, 1¾ × 1⅝" (4.4 × 4.1 cm).
Gift of the manufacturer

CSS/Winfield
Unique Key Card. 1982
Stainless steel, 3½ × 1½"
(8.9 × 3.8 cm). Gift of the
manufacturer

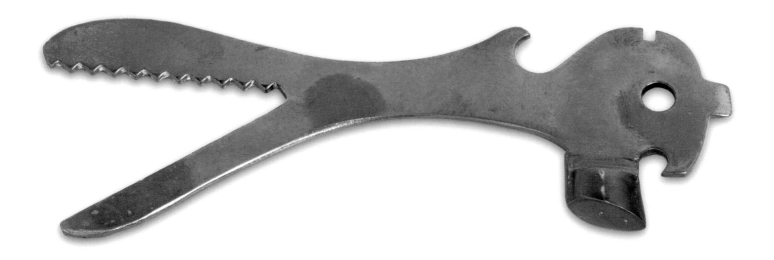

Barcalo Manufacturing Co.
Seven-in-One Tool. c. 1935
Metal with bronze finish, 6½ × 2½ × ½"
(16.5 × 6.4 × 1.3 cm). Gift of Lewis &
Conger

The Stanley Works
Rabbet Plane (no. 93). Before 1900
Nickel-plated steel, 2½ × 6½ × 1"
(6.4 × 16.5 × 2.5 cm). Gift of the
manufacturer

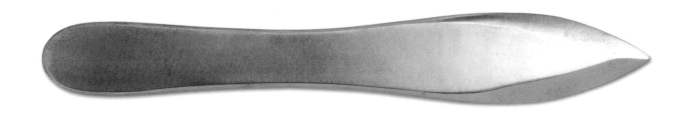

W. D. Randall
Throwing Knife (model 9). c. 1947
Steel, 10" (25.4 cm) long.
Manufacturer: Randall Made Knives,
USA (1966). Gift of the designer

Larry Bamford
Backpacker Hunting Knife. 1973
Stainless steel, 6⅛ × ⅛ × 1⅛"
(15.5 × .3 × 2.8 cm). Manufacturer: Gro
Knives, Inc., USA. Gift of the designer

Carl Elsener
Victorinox Swiss Officer's Knife
Champion (no. 5012). 1968
Plastic and stainless steel,
3⅝ × 1 × 1⅛" (9.2 × 2.5 × 2.9 cm).
Manufacturer: Victorinox, Switzerland
(1976). Gift of Golden West
Merchandisers, USA

The ubiquitous Swiss Officer's Knife is the smallest multi-function tool kit in the world. The pocket knife in the Museum's collection was made by Victorinox, the original producer (but now one of two Swiss companies that make the knives). Victorinox, founded in 1884 by Carl Elsener, manufactures over seven million knives in one hundred different models every year. Each model is named and tailored for its user: the Huntsman, the Electrician, the Executive, the Motorist, and the Lady Swiss are only a few models that incorporate specific tools designed to meet particular needs. Weighing only 7.4 ounces, the Champion has sixteen blades and attachments that perform twenty-nine functions, all in one compact red handle inlaid with the official white cross of Helvetia. The Champion undergoes 450 individual processes during production. The knife's ingenious mechanism allows multiple uses of only eight springs and twenty-four pressure points, which together provide a total spring pressure of 660 pounds. The knives are so durable that, even with a lifetime guarantee, Victorinox estimates that not one in ten thousand returns to the factory for repair.

Elsener designed the first Swiss Officer's Knife in 1897 as a soldier's knife for the Swiss army to replace imported German knives. It became standard equipment for the Swiss army, but became famous internationally only after World War II, when United States military canteens began to stock large quantities of the knife for American soldiers, who popularized and renamed it the Swiss Army Knife. —C.L.

Tapio Wirkkala
Incandescent Bulb (model WIR105).
1959
Glass, 5½ × 4" (14 × 10.2 cm) diam.
Manufacturer: Oy Airam Ab, Finland
(c. 1960). Gift of the manufacturer

George Agule and Charles V. Weden
Electronic Tube. 1954
Rhodium-plated copper, other metals, and heat-resistant glass, 34¾ × 8"
(88.3 × 20.3 cm) diam. Manufacturer:
Machlett Laboratories, Inc., USA. Gift
of the manufacturer

Arthur Young
Bell-47D1 Helicopter. 1945
Aluminum, steel, and acrylic plastic,
9' 2¾" × 9' 11" × 42' 8¾" (281.3 × 302 ×
1271.9 cm). Manufacturer: Bell
Helicopter Inc, USA. Marshall Cogan
Purchase Fund

More than three thousand Bell-47D1 helicopters were made in the United States and sold in forty countries between 1946 and 1973, when production ceased. While the Bell-47D1 is a straightforward utilitarian craft, its designer, Arthur Young, who was also a poet and a painter, consciously juxtaposed its transparent plastic bubble with the open structure of its tail boom to create an object whose delicate beauty is inseparable from its efficiency. That the plastic bubble is made in one piece rather than in sections joined by metal seams sets the Bell-47D1 apart from other helicopters. The result is a cleaner, more unified appearance.

The bubble also lends an insect-like appearance to the hovering craft, which generated its nickname, the "bug-eyed helicopter." It seems fitting, then, that one of the principal uses of the vehicle has been for pest control in crop dusting and spraying. It has also been used for traffic surveillance and for the delivery of mail and cargo to remote areas. During the Korean War, it served as an aerial ambulance.

The Bell-47D1 weighs 1,380 pounds. Its maximum speed is 92 miles per hour and its maximum range 194 miles. It can hover like a dragonfly at altitudes up to 10,000 feet. —P.R.

Mallory Industries
3-Dimensionial Cams. 1991
Aluminum and stainless steel,
largest: 2⅞ × 1⅜" (7.3 × 3.5 cm) diam.
(1992). Gift of the manufacturer

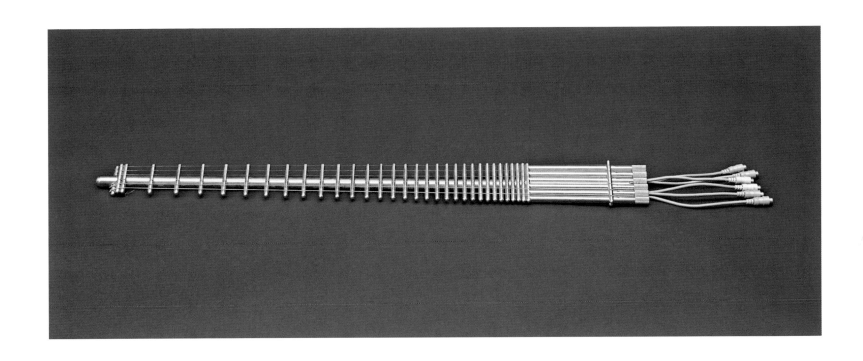

Allan Gittler
Electric Guitar. 1975
Stainless steel, 2½ × 28¾ × 1"
(6.4 × 73 × 2.5 cm). Purchase

International Business Machines Corp.
Control panel for IBM 305 RAMAC
(Random Access Memory Accounting
Machine). 1950
Aluminum frame, aluminum wires,
and plastic, 20¾ × 11¼ × 3"
(52.7 × 28.6 × 7.6 cm). Gift of the
manufacturer

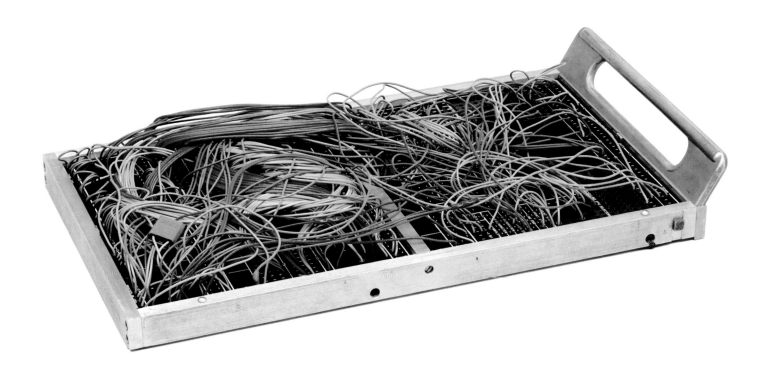

AT&T Bell Laboratories
Diagram of Microprocessor (CRISP).
1986
Computer-generated plot on paper,
172,000 transistors, diagram:
36¼ × 42¾" (92.1 × 108.6 cm).
Gift of the manufacturer

The smallest objects in the Museum's collection are also among the most revolutionary. The integrated circuit, or microchip, signaled the beginning of a new technological era, radically transforming the way we live, work, and communicate. From computers to microwaves, cell phones to satellites, the microchip is the essential component tucked inside the many products that mediate our daily routines. Invented in 1958, the microchip has undergone countless redesigns, as rapid technological advances have allowed for more circuits and transistors to fit into even smaller spaces, making faster, more efficient

chips. In fact, the storable amount of information on a microchip doubles every eighteen months, according to a rule first observed in 1964 by the semiconductor engineer Gordon Moore.

The CRISP chip is represented by a computer-generated image of its circuitry, enlarged five hundred times. The diagram is a two-dimensional design of intricate grids, colors, and lines; the actual chip is a three-dimensional stack of silicon wafers. Each color on the diagram corresponds to a design reduced photographically and etched onto each wafer. The wafers are sliced from a

synthetically grown silicon crystal, using a diamond saw.

The microchip is a paradigm of mass production: tens of thousands are produced each day for only a few cents each. The microchip requires an unparalleled level of precision in the manufacturing process, and is among the most complex designs man has ever made. Although only a computer can decipher the minutiae of these designs, we can intuit their function and appreciate their abstract, rational beauty. This CRISP chip entered the Museum's collection following the 1990 exhibition *Information Art*. —C.L.

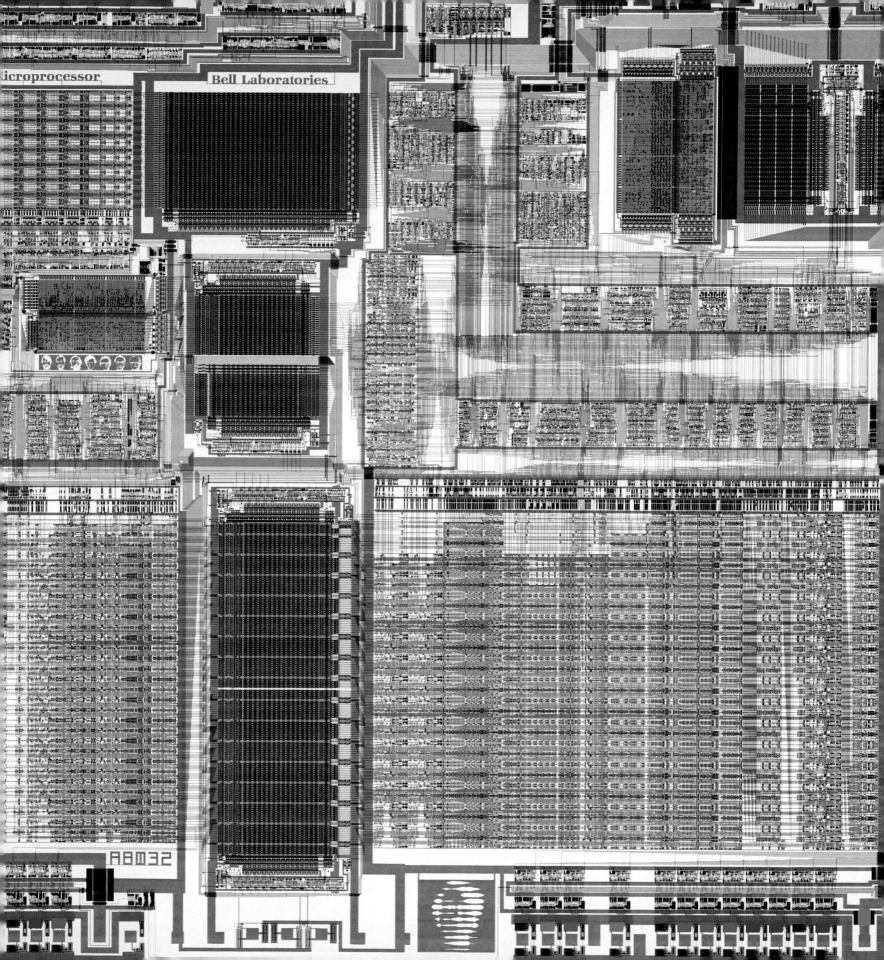

Two years before The Museum of Modern Art was founded in 1929, Alfred H. Barr, Jr., traveled throughout Europe in search of what was new and exciting in the art of his own time. During this trip—on which he saw such wonders of the avant-garde as J. J. P. Oud's architecture in the Netherlands, the Weissenhof Housing Colony in Stuttgart, planned by Ludwig Mies van der Rohe and realized with other major modernist architects, and the work of Aleksandr Rodchenko's Constructivist circle in Moscow—Barr formed many of his most important impressions of modern design as well as art. But, perhaps the most lasting impression—and the one with the greatest consequence to the future Museum—was made by his visit to the Bauhaus in Dessau. Its revolutionary multidisciplinary program in art and design came closest to fulfilling what he envisioned as the promise of modernism.

Individual works produced in the Bauhaus workshops, such as Marianne Brandt's cylindrical nickel-plated Ashtray or Josef Hartwig's abstract geometric Chess Set, greatly appealed to Barr's already established appreciation for simple, spare, and elegant composition. However, what appealed to him most at the Bauhaus was the apparent unity of principles that created a seamless modern world, from typography to tableware, clothing, performance, furniture, art, and architecture. Barr experienced the synthesis of Bauhaus production in all dimensions: seeing Marcel Breuer's experimental tubular-steel furniture being made in Walter Gropius's steel-and-glass workshop building of 1925–26, watching a ballet staged by the Bauhaus students with costumes designed by Oskar Schlemmer, having a meal with Vasily Kandinsky and Paul Klee in one of the Master's houses, also designed by Gropius and furnished with works of art and objects of design created in the Bauhaus shops and studios. For Barr, an important aspect of the Bauhaus and the objects it produced and inspired was the idea that the fine arts and the so-called useful arts could be brought together and that the same high level of discourse could be applied to both.

While a number of Barr's fellow students at Harvard, where he completed his graduate studies in art history, had been unduly burdened by Oswald Spengler's gloomy predictions that Western civilization had run its course, he and Philip Johnson, who visited the Bauhaus in 1929, found irrefutable evidence to the contrary: there they had seen pioneering modern designers experimenting with new materials, such as aluminum, plywood, heat-resistant as well as conventional materials such as glass, and linoleum, who were fully committed to harnessing the forces of modern production to create products that would dignify the life of the common man. Out of this innovative spirit came such designs as Wilhelm Wagenfeld's clear glass tableware of the 1930s, which turned every tabletop into a Purist still life of simple overlapping lines, and his Table Lamp, designed with Carl J. Jucker, known worldwide as the Bauhaus Lamp, as well as the numerous examples of tubular- and stainless-steel furniture by Breuer and Mies van der Rohe of the late 1920s, many of which are classics still in production.

The same spirit could also be seen in the works of Le Corbusier, Pierre Jeanneret, and Charlotte Perriand, whose collaboration brought forth such seminal achievements in modern design as the adjustable Chaise Longue and the Grand Confort, Petit Modèle Armchair. Eileen Gray's chrome-plated tubular-steel Adjustable Table, designed in Paris by the Irish designer, proved to be a mixture of mechanics and platonic geometry that brought the machine metaphor into the domestic environment. Mies van der Rohe, for a time the director of the Bauhaus, and Lilly Reich never collaborated on a furniture design but their parallel activities inspired one another, producing such masterpieces as his Barcelona Chair and her tubular-steel Garden Table. In equally innovative ways, other designers took traditional means of production and traditional objects and reconceived them for a changed world. Anni Albers's cotton-and-silk wall hangings broke no new technical ground, but created patterns that reflected the underlying logic of the warp and weft of weaving, as well as the dynamic to and fro of the machine's movement. Similarly, René Herbst's Desk is not a monument meant to enshrine a bureaucrat but, rather, to serve as a tool for efficiency: a light steel frame and a cast-glass top support the in-and-out trays for speedy modern work flow and a telephone stand for that all-important modern means of communication.

The modern ideal, captured so well in the production of the Bauhaus, has proven to be a continuing source of inspiration, having re-emerged in the postwar period in the Gute Form movement of the Ulm School as well as The Museum of Modern Art's Good Design exhibition program of the 1950s. Despite the inevitability of new and challenging positions within the design profession, the circumstances that created this ideal remain with us today.

—Terence Riley

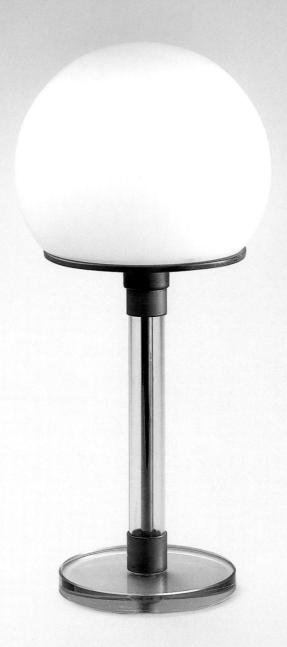

Carl J. Jucker and Wilhelm
Wagenfeld
Table Lamp. 1923–24
Glass and chrome-plated metal,
18 × 8" (45.7 × 20.3 cm) diam.;
5½" (14 cm) diam. at base.
Manufacturer: Bauhaus Metal
Workshop, Germany. Gift of
Philip Johnson

This object, known as the Bauhaus
Table Lamp, embodies the idea *form
follows function*, advanced by the
influential Bauhaus school, which
taught a modern synthesis of both
fine and applied arts. Through the
employment of simple geometric
shapes—circular base, cylindrical
shaft, and spherical shade—Wilhelm
Wagenfeld and Carl J. Jucker
achieved "both maximum simplicity
and, in terms of time and materials,
greatest economy." The lamp's working parts are visible; the opaque
glass shade, a type formerly used
only for industrial lighting, helps to
diffuse the light.

The lamp was produced in the
Bauhaus Metal Workshop after its
re-organization under the direction
of the artist László Moholy-Nagy in
1923. The workshop promoted the
use of new materials and favored
mass production under a collaborative, rather than individual, approach.
Initial attempts at marketing the lamp
in 1924 were unsuccessful, primarily
because most of its parts were still
hand assembled at the Bauhaus.
Today, the lamp is widely produced
by Techno-lumen of Bremen,
Germany, and is generally perceived
as an icon of modern industrial
design. —M.M.

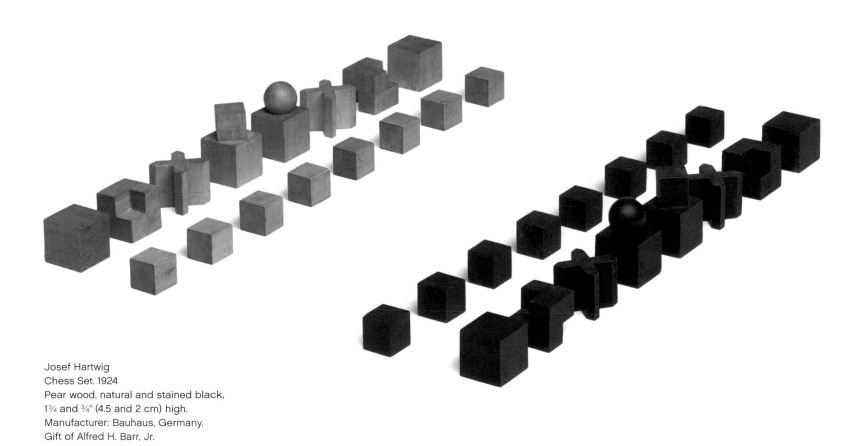

Josef Hartwig
Chess Set. 1924
Pear wood, natural and stained black,
1¾ and ¾" (4.5 and 2 cm) high.
Manufacturer: Bauhaus, Germany.
Gift of Alfred H. Barr, Jr.

Marianne Brandt
Ashtray. 1924
Brass and nickel-plated metal,
2¾ × 3⅛" (7 × 7.9 cm) diam.
Manufacturer: Bauhaus Metal
Workshop, Germany. Gift of John
McAndrew

Marianne Brandt
Hot Water Jug. 1924
Nickel silver, ebony, and raffia,
6⅞ × 3" (17.5 × 7.6 cm) diam.
Manufacturer: Bauhaus Metal
Workshop, Germany. Phyllis B.
Lambert Fund

Marianne Brandt
Table Clock. c. 1930
Painted and chrome-plated metal,
5¾ × 6⅞ × 2¾" (14.6 × 17.5 × 7 cm).
Manufacturer: Ruppelwerk, Germany.
Gift of Jo Carole and Ronald S.
Lauder

"I was never aware that my designs were revolutionary," wrote Marianne Brandt in 1981. "I have simply followed my ideas and the need of the moment." In fact, her designs represent the quintessential philosophy of the Bauhaus Metal Workshop (founded in 1922 by Christian Dell) in which objects were reduced to their purest geometries in order to appear as if mass-produced, a Bauhaus ideal articulated by its founder Walter Gropius in 1923.

The Table Clock shown here—a square face supported by a rectangular pedestal with lines replacing the hours of the day—was designed for the Ruppelwerk metal shop in Gotha during the time Brandt was the head of the Bauhaus Metal Workshop in Dessau. Unlike her teapots, ashtrays, and lamps, this clock is little known, although it seems to be an archetype for the later minimal designs by Braun.

Trained as a painter and sculptor in 1911–18 at the Grand-Ducal Saxon Academy of Fine Art, and later enrolled at the Bauhaus, Weimar, in 1923, Brandt became one of the best-known students of the male-dominated Bauhaus Metal Workshop.

There, László Moholy-Nagy's method of subjecting form and function to critical analysis before designing an object inspired her to develop a lucid formal language that reduced household objects to elemental geometric forms. While she was at the Weimar Bauhaus in 1923–25 and later at Dessau until 1929, Brandt produced some seventy designs, over half of which were lamps. From 1929 to 1930 she worked in Gropius's atelier; in 1933 when the Nazis closed the Bauhaus, she returned to Chemnitz, her birthplace, and later taught painting in Berlin and Dresden. —T.d.C.

Wilhelm Wagenfeld
Pitcher and Saucer. 1932
Heat-resistant glass, two parts:
pitcher 4 × 6 × 3" (10.2 × 15.2 × 7.6 cm)
diam.; saucer ¾ × 6¼" (1.9 × 15.9) diam.
Manufacturer: Jenaer Glaswerk
Schott & Gen., Germany. Gift of Philip
Johnson

Wilhelm Wagenfeld
Heilbronn Bowl. 1937–38
Pressed glass, 3¾ × 8½"
(9.6 × 21.6 cm) diam. Manufacturer:
Vereinigte Lausitzer Glaswerke AG,
Germany. Gift of Manfred Ludewig

Wilhelm Wagenfeld
Kubus Stacking Storage Containers.
1938
Molded glass, largest: 3¼ × 7¼ × 7¼"
(8.3 × 18.4 × 18.4 cm). Manufacturer:
Vereinigte Lausitzer Glaswerke AG,
Germany. Mrs. Armand P. Bartos Fund

Anni Albers
Wall Hanging. 1927
Cotton and silk, 58¼ × 47¾"
(147.9 × 121.3 cm). Manufacturer:
Workshop of Gunta Stölzl,
Switzerland (1964). Gift of the
designer in memory of Greta Daniel

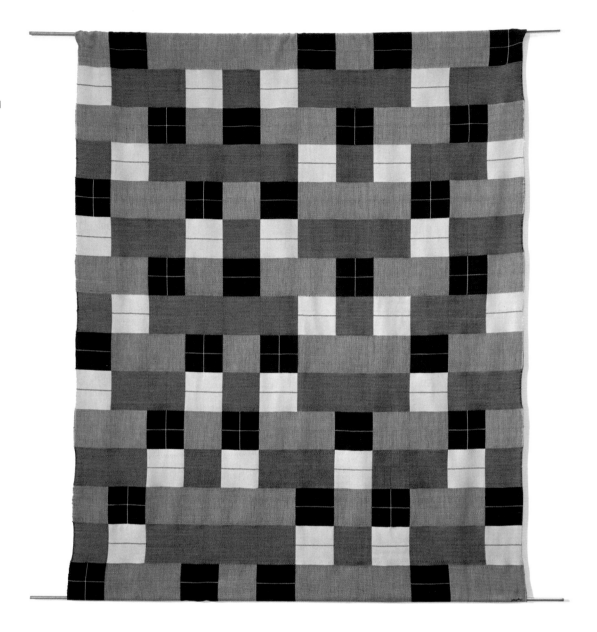

In 1922, when she arrived at the Bauhaus to study art, she was reluctant to join the weaving workshop; yet, while at the Bauhaus, first as student and later as a teacher (and wife of the Bauhaus Master Josef Albers), Anni Albers became one of the most influential textile artists of the twentieth century. Her pioneering approach to textiles created a wide variety of practical materials: wall hangings, rugs, curtain fabrics, upholstery, etc. Their designs were neither pictorial nor referential but, instead, based on geometric abstract patterns, and showed the influence of her instructor Gunta Stölzl and the new abstraction of such artists as Piet Mondrian and Paul Klee.

This Wall Hanging is typical of work that Albers did during her Bauhaus years and reflects her development of the idea of the thread as a carrier of meaning. She created woven pieces that incorporated semantic and artistic elements, such as pictographs, calligraphy, and ideographs, as well as weavings inspired by the ancient peoples of the Andes. Albers's original 1927 watercolor design, used to create this example of her work, served as a maquette for four other textiles as well, all made in 1964 in the Stölzl workshop with the designer's approval.

Albers also influenced the course of fabric making itself by introducing new fibers and finishes and deriving patterns from the structure of woven cloth. Traditional natural materials are often combined with synthetics, such as rayon, cellophane, and metallic thread, to reveal the essential and contrasting characteristics of the materials. In 1933, after the Gestapo padlocked the doors of the Bauhaus, Anni and Josef Albers emigrated to the United States. The Museum of Modern Art honored her in 1949 with its first exhibition dedicated to a weaver, *Anni Albers: Textiles*, and holds one of the finest collections of her work. —B.C.

Eileen Gray
Screen. 1922
Lacquered wood and brass rods,
74½ × 53½ × ¾" (189.2 × 135.9 × 1.9 cm).
Hector Guimard Fund

This black lacquered wood screen, composed of seven horizontal rows of panels joined by thin vertical metal rods, is not only a movable wall that serves to demarcate space but also a sculpture composed of solids and voids with an underlying Cubist influence. It is one of the most striking and elegant creations by Eileen Gray, who was one of the leading designers working in Paris after World War I. Gray popularized and perfected the art of lacquered furnishings, and her preference for its meticulous finish reveals a predilection for exotic materials, in particular those used in Japanese decorative arts.

Based on a larger version that Gray designed in 1922 for the Paris apartment of Madame Mathieu-Lévy, the owner of an exclusive millinery shop, the freestanding block screen can be seen as a bridge between furniture, architecture, and sculpture. Gray also became an accomplished textile designer and architect. Her first major architectural project, the E-1027 House in Roquebrune-Cap-Martin, France, was composed of multifunctional rooms and furniture, and was much admired by Le Corbusier. The flexibility inherent in this project continued Gray's fascination in her earlier designs with pivoting parts and movable elements that transform both object and space.
—M.M.

Eileen Gray
Adjustable Table. 1927
Chrome-plated tubular steel, sheet
steel, and glass, variable: 21¼ to 36½ ×
20" (54 to 93 × 50.8 cm) diam.
Manufacturer: Aram Designs Ltd.,
England (1976). Philip Johnson Fund
and Aram Designs Ltd., London

Eileen Gray
Tube Lamp. c. 1930s
Chrome-plated steel and
incandescent tube, 36 × 9⅞"
(91.5 × 25.1 cm) diam. Estée and
Joseph Lauder Design Fund

Le Corbusier (Charles-Édouard Jeanneret), Pierre Jeanneret, and Charlotte Perriand
Chaise Longue (LC/4). 1928
Chrome-plated steel, fabric, and leather, 26 3/8 × 23 × 62 3/8" (67 × 58.4 × 158.4 cm). Manufacturer: Thonet Frères, France. Gift of Thonet Industries, Inc.

Le Corbusier referred to his furniture as "machines for sitting in," just as he had referred to the house as a "machine for living in" in his 1923 manifesto *Towards a New Architecture*. The Chaise Longue, designed a year after he had begun collaborating with Charlotte Perriand and his cousin Pierre Jeanneret, adapted the tubular steel first used by Marcel Breuer in 1925. It reinterpreted a nineteenth-century tradition with a twentieth-century vocabulary: mobility, a machine-like aesthetic, and ergonomic considerations. According to Perriand, the incline of the curved

frame was designed with a soldier at rest under a tree in mind. Sitting on an independent, fixed steel base, its position responds freely to the needs of the human back through the shifting of weight. The neck roll, secured by a strap, is similarly adjustable, allowing various potential positions for an individual of any size. The base, H-shaped in elevation and elliptical in section, is reminiscent of the aerodynamically designed wing struts of an Henri Farman airplane, which—along with the car and ocean liner—was Le Corbusier's esteemed symbol of the movement

and speed of the industrial age.

The first models of this chair were not produced with one continuous piece of steel but, rather, had sturdy top and bottom bars. Hence, the model shown here, while a 1928 design, reflects a later modification made by the manufacturer in the early 1930s. Ironically, while Le Corbusier's design seems to epitomize the mass production of the industrial age through its use of materials and structure, unlike the chairs of Breuer and others, its complex design made it extremely costly to reproduce. —T.d.C.

Charlotte Perriand
Revolving Armchair. 1928
Chrome-plated steel and leather,
29¾ × 22 × 21¼" (75.6 × 55.9 × 54 cm).
Manufacturer: Thonet Frères, France
(1929). Gift of Thonet Industries, Inc.

Le Corbusier (Charles-Édouard
Jeanneret), Pierre Jeanneret, and
Charlotte Perriand
Grand Confort, Petit Modèle
Armchair. 1928
Chrome-plated steel, horsehair,
down, and leather, 26 × 30 × 27¾"
(66 × 76.2 × 70.5 cm). Manufacturer:
Heidi Weber, Switzerland (1959). Gift
of Phyllis B. Lambert

Jean Prouvé
Folding Chair. 1924
Steel and linen, 40⅜ × 17⅝ × 18¾"
(102.6 × 44.8 × 47.6 cm). Gift of Jo
Carole and Ronald S. Lauder

René Herbst
Desk. c. 1925
Steel and glass, 32 × 79 × 32½"
(81.3 × 200.7 × 82.6 cm). Gift of
Jo Carole and Ronald S. Lauder and
Mrs. S. I. Newhouse, Jr. Purchase
Fund

René Herbst, along with other designers based in France in the 1920s, such as Eileen Gray, Charlotte Perriand, and Robert Mallet-Stevens, encouraged stripped-down undecorated forms and the use of industrial materials and methods. One of the first French designers to work with flat and tubular steel, Herbst used metal, not commonly accepted for domestic design until after World War II, in his furniture designs as early as 1925.

At the beginning of the twentieth century, machine production's potential to transform virtually every aspect of society was widely seen as revolutionary, and the language of the machine itself was translated into objects such as this desk. Glass and steel were a radical departure from the fine woods and delicate inlays employed by such established French designers as Émile-Jacques Ruhlmann, Louis Süe, and André Mare. With its plain top, black frame, integrated lamp, and perforated metal in-and-out trays, Herbst had pared the desk down to its essential parts, creating an object that reflects its function while also suggesting structural building components.

Trained as an architect, Herbst ran practices in London and Frankfurt before establishing himself in Paris. He was awarded a diploma of honor for his furniture at the Paris Exposition Internationale des Arts Décoratifs et Industriels of 1925. Three years later, however, his display of nickel-plated and bent tubular-steel furniture at the Salon des Artistes Décorateurs, secured him a place among the avant-garde generation concerned largely with an aesthetic of the machine.—B.C.

Marcel Breuer
Folding Armchair (model B4). 1927
Chrome-plated tubular steel and
eisengarn fabric, 27⅞ × 30⅞ × 25"
(70.8 × 78.4 × 63.5 cm). Manufacturer:
TECTA Möbel, Germany (1980). Gift of
Maximilian A. Sepp Ltd.

Marcel Breuer
Wassily Chair. 1927–28
Chrome-plated tubular steel and
canvas, 28¼ × 30¾ × 28"
(71.8 × 78.1 × 71.1 cm). Manufacturer:
Standard Möbel, Germany. Gift of
Herbert Bayer

While teaching at the Bauhaus, Marcel Breuer often rode a bicycle, a pastime that led him to what is perhaps the single most important innovation in furniture design in the twentieth century: the use of tubular steel. The tubular steel of his bicycle's handlebars was strong and lightweight, and lent itself to mass production. Breuer reasoned that if it could be bent into handlebars, it could be bent into furniture forms.

The model for this chair is the traditional overstuffed club chair; yet all that remains is its mere outline, an elegant composition traced in gleaming steel. The canvas seat, back, and arms seem to float in space. The body of the sitter does not touch the steel framework. Breuer spoke of the chair as "my most extreme work . . . the least artistic, the most logical, the least 'cozy' and the most mechanical." What he might have added is that it

was also his most influential work. Breuer designed an earlier version of this chair in 1925, and within a year, designers everywhere were experimenting with tubular steel, which would take furniture into a radically new direction. The chair became known as the Wassily after the painter Kandinsky, Breuer's friend and fellow Bauhaus instructor, who praised the design when it was first produced. —P.R.

Marcel Breuer
Stool (model B37). 1932
Chrome-plated tubular steel and
eisengarn fabric, 18 × 18 × 19½"
(45.7 × 45.7 × 49.5 cm). Manufacturer:
Gebrüder Thonet AG, Germany.
Marcel Breuer Purchase Fund

Marcel Breuer
Tea Cart (model B54). 1928
Bent nickel-plated tubular steel,
wood, and linoleum, 30½ × 34⅝ × 21½"
(77.5 × 88 × 54.6 cm). Manufacturer:
Gebrüder Thonet, Austria. Estée and
Joseph Lauder Design Fund

Marcel Breuer
Nesting Tables (model B9). 1925–26
Tubular steel and lacquered plywood,
various dimensions, largest:
23⅞ × 26 × 15¼" (60.7 × 66 × 38.7 cm).
Manufacturer: Gebrüder Thonet,
Austria. Gift of Dr. Anny Baumann

Marcel Breuer
Table (model B10). 1927
Tubular steel and wood, 26¼ ×
29⅛ × 29⅛" (66.7 × 74 × 74 cm).
Manufacturer: Gebrüder Thonet,
Austria. Philip Johnson Fund

Ludwig Mies van der Rohe
Column from the German Pavilion,
International Exposition, Barcelona,
Spain. 1928–29
Metal cladding, 118½ × 16¼ × 15¼"
(301 × 41.3 × 38.7 cm). Purchase

Ludwig Mies van der Rohe
Barcelona Chair. 1929
Stainless-steel bars and leather
upholstery, 31 × 29⅜ × 30"
(78.7 × 74.6 × 76.2 cm). Manufacturer:
Knoll International, Inc., USA (1953).
Gift of the manufacturer

The Barcelona Chair achieves the
serenity of line and the refinement
of proportions and materials characteristic of Ludwig Mies van der
Rohe's highly disciplined architecture. It is supported on each side by
two chrome-plated, flat steel bars.
Seen from the side, the single curve
of the bar forming the chair's back
and front legs crosses the S-curve
of the bar forming the seat and
back legs, making an intersection
of the two. This simple shape
derives from a long history of

precedents, from ancient Egyptian
folding stools to nineteenth-century
neoclassical seating. The can-
tilevered seat and the back of the
original chairs were upholstered in
white kid leather with welt-and-
button details.

Mies van der Rohe designed this
chair for his German Pavilion at the
Barcelona Exposition of 1929. The
Pavilion was the site of the inaugu-
ral ceremony for the German
exhibits at the exposition, and the
Spanish king was to preside. It had

to be an "important chair, a very
elegant chair," according to the
architect. "The government was
to receive a king . . . the chair had to
be . . . monumental. In those circumstances, you just couldn't use
a kitchen chair."

Although only two Barcelona
chairs were made for the German
Pavilion, the design was put into production and became so popular that,
with the exception of one sixteen-
year period, it has been manufactured since 1929. —P.R.

Ludwig Mies van der Rohe
Brno Chair. 1929–30
Chrome-plated steel and leather,
31½ × 23 × 24" (80 × 58.4 × 61 cm).
Manufacturer: Knoll International, Inc.,
USA. Gift of the manufacturer

Hans and Wassili Luckhardt
Side Chair (model ST14). 1931
Tubular steel and molded plywood,
$34\frac{5}{8} \times 21\frac{3}{16} \times 24\frac{3}{16}$" (88 × 53.8 × 61.5 cm).
Manufacturer: Deutsche Stahlmöbel
(DESTA), Germany. Purchase

Ludwig Mies van der Rohe
MR Coffee Table. 1927
Chrome-plated tubular steel and
glass, 19¾ × 29" (50.2 × 73.7 cm) diam.
Manufacturer: Knoll International, Inc.,
USA (1976). Gift of the manufacturer

Ludwig Mies van der Rohe
Tugendhat Coffee Table. 1930
Stainless steel and plate glass,
18 × 40 × 40" (45.7 × 101.6 × 101.6 cm).
Manufacturer: Knoll International, Inc.,
USA (1948). Phyllis B. Lambert Fund

Lilly Reich
Garden Table (LR500). 1931
Tubular steel, enamel, and beech
veneer, 27⅝ × 27" (70.8 × 68.7 cm) diam.
Manufacturer: Shea & Latone, Inc.,
USA (1996). Gift of the manufacturer

Lilly Reich's Garden Table is one of a series of tubular-steel designs that were brought back into production, using her original drawings, on the occasion of the Museum's 1996 exhibition, *Lilly Reich: Designer and Architect*. It is an elegant design in which the tubular steel is gracefully bowed into three legs that have an air of lightness and balance. The red enamel adds warmth and color in place of the steel's customary cold and bright chrome-plated surface. Although Reich refines the plywood tabletop with a final layer of beech veneer, she makes no attempt to conceal its simple construction. The table looks as fresh and contemporary today as it did in 1931 when it was first set into production by Bamberg Metallwerkstätten, Berlin.

Reich, together with her contemporaries Eileen Gray, Marianne Brandt, and Charlotte Perriand, was a pioneering woman in design. In 1920 she became the first woman on the board of directors of the Deutscher Werkbund (German Work Federation), an organization that promoted and upheld the highest standards in German design and manufacture. Only a few women of her generation obtained teaching positions in art schools; nevertheless, Reich held the post of director of the weaving and interiors workshops at the Bauhaus. Her work as a designer of interiors, industrial objects, and exhibitions bespeaks a unique talent that has been overshadowed by her partnership with Ludwig Mies van der Rohe. Reich and Mies often worked together on exhibition designs, and they maintained separate studios. The Museum's exhibition of her work acknowledged Reich as a designer in her own right and recognized her important contributions to the field.—C.L.

4 | Useful Objects

n 1938, the Museum teamed up with retailers to exhibit recent designs that were affordable to the average consumer. The exhibition's title was *Useful Household Objects under $5.00*, and it consisted of well-designed objects, ranging from kitchen utensils, traveling bathroom accessories to glassware, wall coverings, and curtains, all for under $5.00. It was shown in seven other cities in addition to New York, at venues ranging from colleges and department stores to small specialty shops. The objects were selected by the curator John McAndrew according to their suitability of purpose, material, and process of manufacture. The exhibition was so successful and had such a positive response that an annual series of Useful Objects exhibitions followed. It lasted for nine years, until 1947; and while the term *useful* remained constant, the price increased over the years (to $100 dollars in 1947). In other shows the objects reflected the war years, for example, those chosen for the 1942 *Useful Objects in Wartime under $10* exhibition avoided objects made of materials integral to the war effort: metals, plastics such as Lucite, Plexiglas, nylon, Bakelite, and crystallites (used in airplanes and other military equipment), and leather.

While the aesthetic celebrated by the Museum's 1934 *Machine Art* exhibition came to define the design collection early on, the term *useful objects* actually had appeared a year prior, in the 1933 exhibition *Objects: 1900 and Today*. This, the Museum's first design show, was both a contemporary survey and an historical retrospective, which contrasted the vast differences between design at the turn of the century, such as the handicrafts of William Morris and the natural forms of Art Nouveau, and that witnessed by the "modern" 1930s. The curator Philip Johnson juxtaposed the terms *decorative* and *useful* in comparing the two different attitudes toward design: one based "on the imitation of natural forms and lines which curve, diverge and converge," and another based on utility, the

modern mindset "that industrial design is functionally motivated and follows the same principles as modern architecture: machine-like simplicity, smoothness of surface, avoidance of ornament."

Unlike the objects included in *Machine Art,* the useful objects presented here are not collected primarily for their purity of form but, rather, for the integration of an innovative functionality and often the use of new materials. In other words, in the case of useful objects, form, and ultimately beauty, follows function. Products such as the folding flashlight, the ergonomic designs for a fork-spoon, interlocking bottles, or the collapsible hexagonal salad basket modify established forms to improve performance. The Glass Frying Pan and Baking Dish, for example, were not only direct responses to innovations in glass (Pyrex, or heat-resistant borosilicate glass), but arose out of the war effort to reduce the use of metal in kitchen appliances. Likewise, the lightweight materials of the Racing Wheelchair not only adapt innovations from the aerospace industry but reflect an attitude influenced by politics, an awareness of the equal rights of minority groups. Even the Cable Turtles, made of thermoplastic elastomers, a form of plastic that is recyclable, responded to the need for "green" products in an expanding technological world, in which cords tangle up our desks and homes. It was such utility and convenience that was touted in the original exhibitions in the hope of improving lifestyles and daily routines.

Perhaps the most influential innovation to result directly in a rethinking of standard objects, however, has been that in plastics. The use of Bakelite, the first synthetic material, in the late 1920s and early 1930s for electrical goods and automobile parts because of its superior insulating properties and rigidity, resulted in a radical modification of the Electric Hairdryer. Its earlier brass and metal counterpart is surprisingly pared down to a handle, motor, and airshaft, a form that endures today. PVC (vinyl), melamine, poly-

ethylene, polystyrene, and nylon, all were invented in the 1930s, but did not enter the consumer market until the 1950s owing to the war effort. They had a revolutionary effect. Everything from Tupperware, one of the earliest products to employ polyethylene, to its myriad variations, such as the blow-molded Container for Liquids, exploited its toughness at low temperatures and its low production costs. Likewise, other plastics and techniques refined in the 1950s, such as ABS and injection molding, were adapted in the functional household object and in the purely pleasurable arena of toy design. By 1958, LEGO became the first Danish toy company to employ refined processes of injection molding, and their trademark "stud-and-tube" coupling system of plastic bricks, heretofore made of wood, took hold.

From the 1960s to today, expanded-polyurethane foams, wet-look polyurethane, glossy ABS, transparent acrylic, and thermoplastic elastomers have not only transformed the domestic landscape, but have come to reflect an increasingly transient, disposable, and impermanent lifestyle. The collapsible and lightweight baby stroller made of Polythene (Dupont's brand of polyethylene), the Spoon Straw and the Disposable Folder Razor are no longer solely useful objects for the home but for consumers who are increasingly mobile.

The Useful Objects series celebrated the ideal of standardization to make good design universally available. The first exhibition was a testament to the democratic notion that good or useful design did not have to be expensive, and a belief that aesthetically functional objects should be available to all. With the invention of plastics and disposable products, this pursuit seemed more feasible than ever. In subsequent exhibitions, while the term *useful objects* has not been used explicitly, the premise of utility has been a forceful presence.

—Tina di Carlo

Designer unknown
Electric Hairdryer. c. 1928
Nickel-plated metal, wood, and
Bakelite resin, 8¾ × 5 × 9⅜"
(22.3 × 12.7 × 23.8 cm). Manufacturer:
Friho-sol, Germany. Marshall Cogan
Purchase Fund

Christopher Dresser
Watering Can. c. 1876
Painted tin, 12⅝ × 9⅞ × 7¼"
(32 × 25.1 × 18.4 cm). Manufacturer:
Richard Perry, Son & Co., England
(c. 1884). Gift of Paul F. Walter

Designer unknown
Welder's Mask. Before 1930
Coated cardboard, glass, Bakelite
resin, and metal, 9 × 9 × 7"
(22.9 × 22.9 × 17.8 cm). Manufacturer:
American Optical Corp., USA (c. 1930).
Department Purchase Fund

Corning Glass Works
Frying Pan. n.d.
Borosilicate glass and steel,
2¾ × 12½" (7 × 31.8 cm). Purchase

Designer unknown
Tumbler. Before 1947
Glass, 4¾ × 2⅝" (12.1 × 6.7 cm) diam.
Manufacturer: American. Purchase

98

The Stanley Works
Tinsmith's Hammer. Before 1940
Steel and wood, 12 × 4⅜ × 1"
(30.5 × 11.1 × 2.5 cm). Purchase

Corning Glass Works
Baking Dish. 1949
Borosilicate glass, 2¼ × 10⅛ × 8⅝"
(5.7 × 25.7 × 21.9 cm). Gift of Greta
Daniel

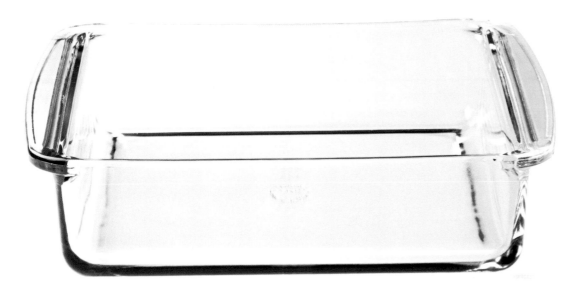

Vernon P. Steele
Adjustable Garden Rake. 1945
Aluminum and wood, 64⅜ × 22¾"
(163.5 × 57.8 cm). Manufacturer: Kenco
Products Corp., USA (c. 1945–48).
Purchase

Ikkan Hiki
Chasen. Before 1953
Bamboo, 4½ × 2¼" (11.5 × 5.7 cm)
diam. Gift of Japan

Charles B. Kaufmann
Bird Control Strips. 1949
Stainless steel, each: 3¾ × 4 × 2"
(9.5 × 10.2 × 5.1 cm). Manufacturer:
Nixalite of America, USA (1950).
Gift of the manufacturer

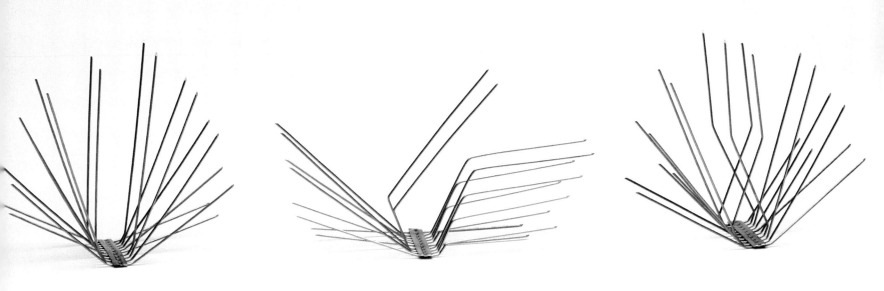

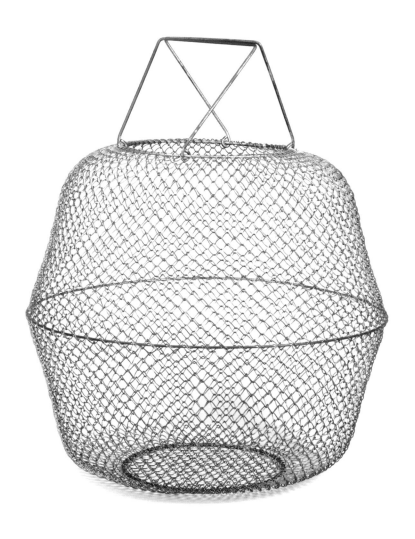

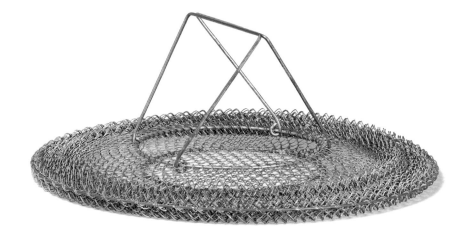

Designer unknown
Collapsible Salad Basket. Before 1953
Tinned steel, 19 × 16" (48.3 × 40.6 cm)
diam. at center. Manufacturer:
H. A. Mack & Co., USA. Gift of the
manufacturer

Harry V. Cremonese
Delphic Kitchen Utility Blades. 1973
Carbon stainless steel and beech
wood, various dimensions, largest:
15 × 3⅜ × ¾" (38.1 × 8.6 × 1.9 cm).
Manufacturer: Mitsuboshi Co., Japan
(1975). Gift of the designer

Peter Sciascin
Lobster Pick. n.d.
Plastic and stainless steel, 8¼ × ¾"
(21 × 1.9 cm). Manufacturer: Holt
Howard Associates, USA (1954).
Purchase

John Hays Hammond
Bottle Opener. 1948
Bronze and magnetic top, 6¼ × ⅝"
(15.9 × 1.6 cm). Manufacturer:
Hammond Research Corp., USA.
Gift of the manufacturer

Earl Silas Tupper
Pitcher and Creamer. 1946
Polyethylene, pitcher 6½ × 6⅝ × 4¾"
(16.5 × 16.8 × 12.1 cm); creamer
4¼ × 4¼ × 3³⁄₁₆" (10.8 × 10.8 × 8.1 cm).
Manufacturer: Tupper Corporation,
USA (c. 1954). Gift of the manufacturer

In the early 1940s, Earl Silas Tupper, a chemist and a designer of metal corsets and garter belts, started experimenting with injection-molded polyethylene, a new industrial material used primarily for insulation, radar, and radio equipment. In 1942 he founded the Tupper Corporation to manufacture household items out of the new material. The first designs, released in 1946, included a coffee cup with a handle integrated into the body of the cup and tumblers with flowered edges for easier sipping.

The following year, Tupper applied for a patent for what turned out to be his landmark invention, the Tupper Seal, an airtight polyethylene closure based on that of a paint can. Using this ingenious system, he began to manufacture the semi-opaque, pastel-colored stackable food containers that came to epitomize 1950s suburban American life. The containers (designed, according to Tupper, to make a "woman's life" easier) were heralded for their economic and innovative design. *House Beautiful* referred to them as "fine art for 39 cents," and compared the "gorgeous" material to alabaster and jade, but they did not sell well. Then in 1951 Tupper hired Brownie Wise, a middle-aged, divorced mother who correctly decided that throwing a party for neighboring housewives was the best way to sell plastic. In 1958 the Tupper Corporation was sold to the Rexall Drug Company after Tupper had a falling out with Wise. Rexall promptly renamed the company and its products, Tupperware, a name that still conjures up a postwar consumer culture of standardization, self-service, and efficiency.

Although a clearer and less wax-like form of polyethylene was used beginning in the 1960s, the material of the original containers has deteriorated rapidly, prompting museum curators and conservators worldwide to devise new solutions for the upkeep of twentieth-century innovative materials. —T.d.C.

Juris Mednis
Bottles. 1983
Polyethylene plastic, each:
8¾ × 2⅞ × 2¼" (22.2 × 7.3 × 5.7 cm).
Gift of the designer

Willys-Overland Motors, Inc.
Truck: Utility ¼ Ton 4 × 4 (M38A1)
Jeep. 1952
Steel body, 6' 1¾" × 60⅞" × 11' 6⅝"
(187.3 × 154.6 × 352.1 cm). Gift of
DaimlerChrysler Corporation Fund

The Jeep is the quintessential utilitarian vehicle—a reliable tool whose primary function is transport, on or off road. Its official name, Truck: Utility 1/4 Ton 4 x 4, means it is a four-wheel-drive vehicle capable of carrying 500 pounds. The origin of its popular name, Jeep, has been much debated.

The Jeep was first invented in 1940, when the United States Army issued specifications for a small, powerful, general-purpose vehicle. Engineers from the American Bantam Car Company, Ford Motor Company, and Willys-Overland Motors, Inc. were largely responsible for designing the Jeep in a matter of weeks for the Army, a supreme example of American engineering ingenuity. The Jeep was one of the most technolog-

Roberto Menghi
Container for Liquids. 1958
Polyethylene plastic, 19 × 14 × 6"
(48.3 × 35.6 × 15.2 cm). Manufacturer:
Pirelli, Italy. Gift of the manufacturer

ically advanced machines at the time. After World War II, Willys-Overland Motors continued to produce the Jeep for military and civilian markets.

In 1952 engineers at Willys-Overland modified the original 1940 design and produced the M38A1, a new model that was faster, slightly larger, and widely considered to be the best military Jeep ever built. Like the original model on which it is based, it is characterized by a flat body with high ground clearance, yet with a low overall height. When the Museum first exhibited a Jeep in 1951, the curator Arthur Drexler described it as "a sturdy sardine can on wheels." The profile resembles a metal box, but with good reason. The flat body rides high above the ground for clearance over rough terrain. The Jeep's overall height remains low for strategic reasons. Even the windshield can be folded down on the hood. The absence of side doors makes it easy to get in or out quickly. Only a canvas canopy provides shelter from rain. With the wheels removed, the boxlike bodies could be efficiently crated and stacked for shipment. The M38A1, with its curved hood and fenders and its distinctive front grille panel, remained in production for sixteen years and strongly influenced the design of popular civilian Jeeps for more than three decades—a testament to its functional appeal and its transformation into a cultural icon. —P.R.

O. F. Maclaren
Baby Stroller. 1966
Aluminum alloy tubing and
polyethylene fabric, 35 × 15 × 36"
(88.9 × 38.1 × 91.5 cm). Manufacturer:
Andrew Maclaren Ltd., England (1967).
Gift of the designer

Godtfred Kirk Christiansen
LEGO Building Bricks. 1954–58
ABS plastic, various dimensions,
largest: 7/16 × 1¼ × 5/8" (1.1 × 3.2 × 1.6 cm).
Manufacturer: LEGO Group, Denmark
(1958). Gift of the manufacturer

Godtfred Kirk Christiansen, whose
father founded LEGO, believed that
play is a process of discovery and
learning that is essential to a child's
growth and development. LEGO
Building Bricks offer unlimited possibilities for creative and imaginative
play. These miniature modular elements, in various sizes, shapes, and
colors, have inspired children of all
ages to construct three-dimensional
play environments, from pirate ships

and underwater worlds to castles
and spacecraft. Recent developments include interactive software, a
story-driven building universe, and
robotics programming and construction. LEGO has even developed a
business-strategy building system for
adults called LEGO Serious Play.

Founded in 1932, the LEGO Group
originally produced wood toys for
children. The company name derives
from the Danish *leg godt*, which

means "play well." The current plastic
bricks, with their stud-and-tube
coupling system, were introduced in
1958. The first bricks were made of
cellulose acetate, later replaced with
acrylonitrile butadiene styrene (ABS),
a more stable plastic with better
color quality. LEGO estimates that
over the past sixty years, its global
sales translate into the equivalent of
fifty-two blocks for each of the
world's six billion inhabitants. —C.L.

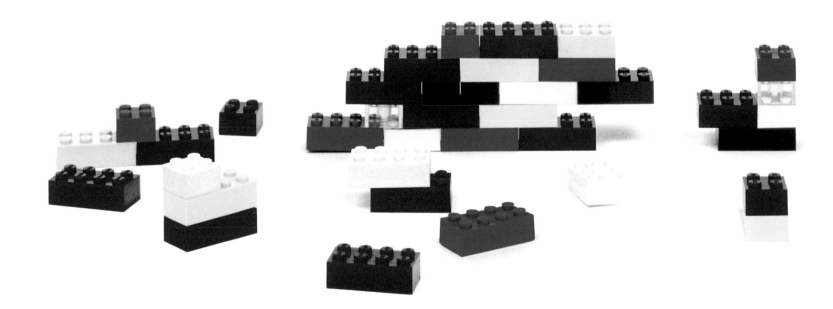

Russell Manoy
Mug and Plate. 1966–67
Melamine resin, plate 11 × 7 × 1¾"
(27.9 × 17.8 × 4.4 cm); mug 5 × 2¾"
(12.7 × 7cm) diam. Manufacturer:
Antiference Ltd., England. Gift of
Lumex, Inc.

Ergonomi Design Gruppen, Maria
Benktzon, and Sven-Eric Juhlin
Knork Fork. 1978
Polycarbonate and ABS plastics and
stainless steel, 7¼ × 1¼ × ¾"
(18.4 × 3.2 × 1.9 cm). Manufacturer:
RFSU Rehab, Sweden (1980). Gift of
the manufacturer

Ergonomi Design Gruppen, Maria
Benktzon, Håkan Bergkvist, and
Sven-Eric Juhlin
Adjustable Spoons. 1986
Polycarbonate and ABS plastics,
each: 6½ × 1⅜" (16.5 × 3.5 cm).
Manufacturer: RFSU Rehab, Sweden
(1990). Gift of the manufacturer

Britt-Louise Sundell
Mixing Bowl. 1960
Propen plastic, 5⅜ × 10¾ × 11½"
(13.7 × 27.3 × 29.2 cm). Manufacturer:
Gustavsberg, Sweden. Gift of Design
Research

Richard Sapper
Espresso Coffee Maker (model
9090). 1978
Steel, 8 × 6 × 4⅞" (20.3 × 15.2 × 12.4 cm)
diam. Manufacturer: Alessi, Italy.
Gift of the manufacturer

Richard Sapper
Minitimer Kitchen Timer. 1971
Plastic, 1⅛ × 2⅝" (2.8 × 6.7 cm) diam.
Manufacturer: Ritz-Italora, Italy. Gift of
the Terraillon Corporation

Smart Design
Good Grips Paring Knife. 1989
Stainless steel and synthetic rubber,
7¾ × 1⅜ × 1" (19.7 × 3.5 × 2.5 cm).
Manufacturer: Oxo International, USA
(c. 1990). Gift of the designers

Herbert Allen
Screwpull Corkscrew. 1979
Polycarbonate plastic and metal,
5¾ × 3 × 1⅛" (14.6 × 7.6 × 2.9 cm).
Manufacturer: Hallen Co., USA (1981).
Gift of the manufacturer

The wine-lover's dream is a hassle-free corkscrew. The Screwpull was invented to satisfy such a dream—to pull even the most recalcitrant cork from its bottle with ease. This efficient low-priced gadget is astonishing in its simplicity. First, its plastic frame is fitted snugly over the bottle's neck. Then the helical screw, with its anti-friction coating, is lowered—by turning the knob at the top—through the guide and driven into the cork. With continued rotation, and without the need to pull, the cork rises out of

the bottle and climbs up the screw until it is removed.

Herbert Allen, a prolific inventor and engineer in the oil-drilling and aerospace industries, designed this infallible tool. During his first trip to Europe in the 1950s, he became a wine enthusiast. He began work on the Screwpull in 1975 at his wife's request for a corkscrew that would perform perfectly and effortlessly every time. Four years later the corkscrew was available on the market in a range of colors, including clear, white, amber, and black.

Allen defined his philosophy about design as always trying to achieve the best performance. He explained: "The Screwpull is an example of this same philosophy, namely to design a product that would do a given task far more efficiently than anything else available . . . I happen to believe that attention to aesthetic design, as well as the required attention to the functional design, leads to a superior ultimate design." Indeed, the Screwpull transcends mere function with its outstanding aesthetic characteristics. —P.R.

Eugene Walters
Welding Helmet (model 700). 1980
Fiberglass and plastic, 12½ × 8 × 7½"
(31.8 × 20.3 × 19.1 cm). Manufacturer:
Fibre-Metal Products Co., USA (1982).
Skidmore, Owings & Merrill Design
Fund

The Welding Helmet designed by
Eugene Walters, with its indestructi-
ble and solid appearance, clearly
indicates its use as a barrier against
sparks, fumes, and heat. It features a
broad, spherical oval of fiberglass
specifically designed for welding in
cramped areas. The rectangular
visor, molded into the helmet, adds
to its overall impenetrable character,
filters out infrared and ultraviolet
light, and prevents a debilitating halo
effect from refracted light. The particular fiberglass used here makes for a
lighter, stronger, and more flexible
helmet than previous models. Fibre-
Metal introduced the first welding
helmet made of fiberglass in 1952.
This model was shown in the
Museum's 1991 exhibition *Modern
Masks and Helmets*.

Helmets and masks are often
indispensable protective devices for
the survival of hazardous and
extreme situations, such as warfare,
sports, and industrial labor.
Frequently they are able to transcend their primary role of protection
and serve to disguise or proclaim a
person's identity. Designed to be
expressive as well as protective are
such objects as the goalie mask that
intimidates competitors, the racing
helmet that enhances speed, and the
gas mask that provides ventilation
but also conjures fear and images of
disaster. The Welding Helmet's
machine-made uniformity and industrial look seem to characterize the
wearer as an anonymous, almost
mechanized creature. —C.L.

Emilio Ambasz
Flashlights. 1983
ABS plastic, each: 4 × 1¼ × 1"
(10.2 × 3.2 × 2.5 cm). Manufacturer:
G. B. Plast, Italy (1985). Gift of the
designer

Anthony Maglica
Mag Charger Rechargeable
Flashlight. 1982
Aluminum alloy and borosilicate
glass, 12⅝ × 2⅜" (32.1 × 6 cm) diam.
Manufacturer: Mag Instrument, Inc.,
USA. Gift of the manufacturer

Arthur A. Aykanian
Spoon Straw. 1968
Polypropylene plastic, 8 × ¼"
(20.3 × .6 cm). diam. Manufacturer:
Winkler Flexible Products, Inc., USA
(1979). Gift of the manufacturer

Robert P. Gottlieb
Hairspray Face Protector. 1974
Acrylic plastic, 11¾ × 6⅝ × 1½"
(29.8 × 16.8 × 3.8 cm). Manufacturer:
Two's Company, USA. Gift of the
manufacturer

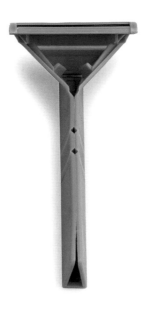

Athos Bergamaschi
Disposable Foldable Razors. 1975
Polypropylene plastic and stainless
steel, each: open, 3¾ × 1¾ × 1⅛"
(9.5 × 4.4 × 2.9 cm); closed,
⅜ × 1¾ × 1¾" (1 × 4.4 × 4.4 cm).
Manufacturer: Elberel Italiana, Italy
(1977). Gift of Domus Academy, Italy

Mark Sanders
No-Spill Chopping Board. 1988
Polypropylene plastic, 2⅝ × 8¾ × 15¼"
(6.7 × 22.2 × 38.7 cm). Manufacturer:
Rubycliff Ltd., England (1990). Gift of
the designer

Bob Hall
Racing Wheelchair. 1986
Steel and nylon, 23⅝ × 25 × 45"
(60 × 63.5 × 114.3 cm). Manufacturer:
Hall's Wheels, USA (1987). Gift of the
designer

The designer Bob Hall was physically disabled at an early age by polio, and required a wheelchair. Undaunted by his condition, in 1975 he pioneered wheelchair racing by participating in the Boston Marathon. At the time he began competing, a racing wheelchair had not yet been designed. Instead, disabled athletes attempted to improve speed by altering their cumbersome everyday wheelchairs. Hall designed his first racing wheelchair in 1978 and founded a new company, Hall's Wheels. There he made handcrafted wheelchairs, measured to fit each individual, that weighed between fourteen and sixteen pounds, about half the weight of the wheelchair Hall had used in his first marathon.

The racing wheelchair introduced innovations that have had an impact on users of every type of wheelchair. This example, manufactured in 1987, features a lightweight frame of aircraft-steel tubing, a speedometer, and a tachometer. The wheels, adapted from racing bicycles, are angled for optimal arm movement and enhanced speed. The red and black coloring lends a sporty, sleek look. The Museum first showed Hall's Racing Wheelchair in the 1989 exhibition *Designs for Independent Living*, which presented outstanding examples of well-designed, mass-produced objects for the elderly and physically disabled. —C.L.

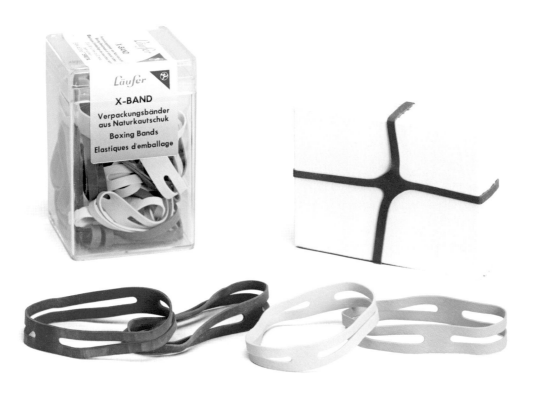

Designer unknown
X-Shaped Rubber Bands. 1995
Synthetic rubber, two sizes: small,
1¾" (4.4 cm) diam.; large, 2¼" (5.7 cm)
diam. Manufacturer: Mahakit Rubber
Co. Ltd., Thailand (1999). Gift of the
supplier, Laufer AC, Germany

Flex Development B.V.
Cable Turtle Cable Spool. 1996
Synthetic rubber, 1¼ × 2½"
(3.2 × 6.4 cm) diam. Manufacturer:
Cleverline, the Netherlands (1997).
Gift of the manufacturer

Décolletage Plastique Design Team
Bic Cristal. 1950
Polystyrene and polypropylene
plastic and tungsten carbide, 5⅞ × ½"
(14.9 × 1.3 cm) diam. Manufacturer:
Société Bic, France. Gift of the
manufacturer

Art Fry and Spencer Silver
Post-it Note. c. 1977
Paper and adhesive, $2\frac{7}{8} \times 2\frac{7}{8}$"
(7.3 × 7.3 cm). Manufacturer: 3M,
USA (1980). Purchase

Among innumerable designs that enrich the Museum's collection, several have had a significant impact on the world. They are usually the ones, like the Bic pen or the Swiss Army knife, that have reached every part of the globe in their original form or in an inspired copy. They are useful, simple, and affordable revolutionary objects that have become necessary.

The Post-it Note is one of them. Many of us cannot imagine life without these "stickies." The original one, featured in the collection, is square to express rationality and yellow to attract attention. The manufacturer has described how its research scientist Dr. Spence Silver had first

developed the technology in 1968 "while looking for ways to improve the acrylate adhesives that 3M uses in many of its tapes. In a classic case of innovative serendipity, Silver found something quite remarkably different from what he was originally looking for. It was an adhesive that formed itself into tiny spheres [each] with a diameter of a paper fiber. The spheres would not dissolve, could not be melted, and were very sticky individually. But because they made only intermittent contact, they did not stick very strongly when coated onto tape backings."

For many years, the application of this new discovery remained

unrealized until Art Fry, a new-product-development researcher at 3M, frustrated with old-fashioned paper bookmarks falling out of books, saw a way to utilize this experimental adhesive, which allowed the removal and reattachment of paper. First a bookmark and soon thereafter an instant memo, the Post-it Note has generated innumerable offshoots and imitations. There even exists a software program, aptly called Stickies, that allows for notes to appear as if stuck onto the computer screen. Yet, it is the original square yellow note that has become ubiquitous in contemporary life. —P.A.

5 | Modern Nature

There is no single idea of nature in modern design. Nature is a cultural construct whose meanings are as varied as its forms. For many designers in the late nineteenth century, nature symbolized freedom, spontaneity, and beauty. The French architect and designer Hector Guimard might have spoken for his entire generation when he wrote about the inexhaustible sources that nature provided: "Let us bend before . . . the examples of the great architect of the universe." Guimard modernized all aspects of design for a cosmopolitan clientele. Every detail of his buildings and their furnishings was infused with his idiosyncratic vision. In drawing inspiration from the vitalistic forms of nature, he created phantasmagoric interiors that evoked the natural world and were a place of retreat from quotidian urban realities.

For many modern designers nature has provided a model and inspiration that facilitated the rejection of tradition and historical revivalism by providing limitless formal and aesthetic possibilities loaded with symbolism and metaphor. Nature has also been considered an antidote to technology, which was perceived to impose an impersonal and unrelenting standardization. But many designs that owe their inspiration to nature are often efficient, structurally logical, and exhibit innovations in form and materials. This is no less true today than a century ago.

When, in 1933, the Museum contrasted contemporary design with fin-de-siècle Art Nouveau, Johnson acknowledged that both the abstract geometric works of the 1920s and the late nineteenth-century works were modern and entirely free from the undesirable tradition of designs based on historical styles. However, he noted: "The earlier designers, unable to invent abstract forms relied on those of nature."

Many enduring works eschewed realism in favor of abstraction. Henry Clemens Van de Velde and August Endell, for example, were less interested in the outward forms of nature than in tapping its inner essence. A free, spontaneous creative act provided an authentic, immediate experience unrestrained by consistency and standardization. Endell described his approach as "the power of form upon the mind, a direct immediate influence without any intermediary stage . . . one of direct empathy." Similarly, Van de Velde, who founded and directed, until World War I began, the famous Kunstgewerbeschule at Weimar (it later became the Bauhaus), vehemently proclaimed the virtues of the creative artist in debate against those who advocated greater standardization: "By his innermost essence the artist is a burning idealist, a free spontaneous creator."

Van de Velde's ideas had a profound effect on subsequent generations of designers, including Alvar Aalto, whose first museum exhibition took place at The Museum of Modern Art in 1938. It showed his innovative bentwood furniture, glass vases, and architecture. One of Aalto's greatest contributions was that he put a human face on technology. Increasingly, he gave priority to the psychosensual aspects of design, forging a remarkable synthesis of romantic and pragmatic ideas, and reflecting his concerns for the common man. This is demonstrated in many ways, including his choice of natural materials, especially birch, and by a design strategy predicated on emotive and associative content which generated an expressive formal vocabulary favoring free form over regularity.

The latent surrealist qualities and freeform designs of Aalto, Frederick Kiesler, and Charles and Ray Eames, among others, were often called *organic*, meant to convey not only naturalist associations but also a totally integrated environment. To that end, the Museum sponsored an international competition in 1940, Organic Design in Home Furnishings. Not surprisingly, there was a renewed interest among designers in the work of Antoni Gaudí, Guimard, and Michael Thonet, which was also reflected in the Museum's exhibition and acquisition program following World War II.

Some designers believed that universal truths could be found in the particulars seen in nature. This strategy often led to a close observation of the local landscape and the use of indigenous materials. For many Finnish designers, such as Tapio Wirkkala, nature practically defined a national design identity, yet their work achieved international recognition and transcended its local origins.

The relationship of materials, process, and technology has played a critical role in the formal evolution of organic design. For instance, the possibilities of bending and laminating wood, explored by Thonet, Aalto, Eames, and others often pushed the material to its limit. The exploration of new synthetic materials, such as plastics and composites, led to a proliferation of organic shapes largely because curvilinear shapes are well suited to, and even enhance, the materials' performance. Computerized manufacturing processes have further liberated designers' imaginations. Organic shapes are now possible in design and architecture that earlier designers only dreamed of achieving, or achieved only through highly individualized hand-made processes. The contemporary relationship between materials and technology was most recently explored at the Museum in the exhibition *Mutant Materials in Contemporary Design* of 1995, which included the MX5 Miata Automobile Taillight as an effective example of this phenomenon.

Among the most compelling new developments in the relationship between design and nature is biomimicry wherein engineers and designers study nature's efficient stratagems in order to create new materials and forms. Nature is considered a source from which to learn rather than a repository of raw materials from which to take. In so doing, biomimicists recognize nature not only for material and formal models, but have rediscovered moral and ecosensitive values in doing so.

—Peter Reed

J. & J. Kohn Co.
Child's Cradle. c. 1895
Ebonized bentwood, 80¼ × 56¼ ×
25⁷⁄₁₆" (203.8 × 142.9 × 64.6 cm).
Gift of Barry Friedman

This elaborate bentwood cradle was lined with thick cushions to create a soft, sheltered, egg-shaped bed for an infant. The sinuous and sensual design, with the elegant, curved forms of the cradle and the long vertical arm that supported draped netting, reflects the popular Art Nouveau style of the time. Such cradles could be found in stylish, bourgeois homes all over Europe.

Bentwood designs became ubiquitous as seating for cafés and gardens and later as elaborate, upholstered domestic furnishings.

Inexpensive, durable, light, and ideal for export because components could be assembled after shipping, pieces such as J. & J. Kohn's cradle became perfect symbols of the new industrial age. The bentwood process was perfected by the German cabinetmaker Michael Thonet in the mid-nineteenth century in order to make appealing functional furniture efficiently and economically. In 1867 the manufacturer J. & J. Kohn became Gebrüder Thonet's chief competitor, opening factories in several international locations. —B.C.

August Endell
Desk Mounts. c. 1899
Wrought iron and wood, 28½ × 34 × 1"
(72.4 × 86.4 × 2.5 cm). Manufacturer:
R. Kirsch, Germany. Acquired by
exchange

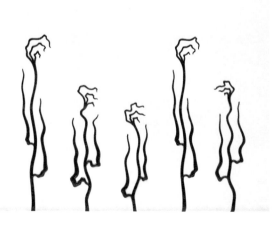

Antoni Gaudí
Grille from the Casa Milà (La Pedrera), Barcelona, Spain. 1906–12 Wrought iron, 65¾ × 73¾ × 19⅝" (167 × 187.3 × 49.8 cm). Gift of H. H. Hecht in honor of George B. Hess and Alice Hess Lowenthal

In the numerous grilles for the semi-basement level of the idiosyncratic Casa Milà, Antoni Gaudí transformed strips of wrought iron into organic, flowing, ribbonlike forms. The mesh patterns evoke images of fishing nets hung out to dry, a common sight on the Mediterranean. The twisting and undulating grille profiles are as much works of abstract sculpture as they are architectural elements. The play between opacity and transparency, strength and plasticity, adds to the variety of organic forms on the facade of the building.

Most of the work of the Catalan architect Gaudí is in Barcelona, the city where he made his home

and participated in every aspect of his buildings. The wildly organic Casa Milà (known as La Pedrera because it was thought to resemble a quarry) is situated on what was then Barcelona's most important thoroughfare, Passeig de Gràcia. Like this grille, the entire building has not a single straight line. Gaudí argued that in nature there is no such thing as a straight line. Nature, from minerals and vegetables to its greatest manifestations of power, was for him an inexhaustible source of inspiration: "The great book, ever open and which we must make every effort to read."

In his quest to find a truly Catalan

regional style, Gaudí created design objects and buildings loosely affiliated with Art Nouveau but which also suggest a bizarre, highly personalized, abstract neo-Gothicism, owing to his interest in the medieval period and his deep Catholic faith. His dreamlike forms, imbued with psychological presence and often evoking notions of dark fantasies (Casa Milà was once rumored to be the Devil's work), influenced artists of the Surrealist movement, particularly his fellow Catalan Salvador Dalí. Other architectural elements from the Casa Milà included in the Museum's collection are ceramic floor tiles and brass doorknobs. —B.C.

125

J. P. Kayser Sohn
Decanter. 1900–02
Pewter, 8 × 3⅝ × 2⅝" (20.3 ×
9.2 × 6.7 cm). Estée and Joseph
Lauder Design Fund

Antoni Gaudí
Prayer Bench. 1898–1914
Wood and wrought iron, 32⅝ ×
44½ × 26" (82.9 × 113 × 66 cm). Estée
and Joseph Lauder Design Fund

Henry Clemens Van de Velde
Lobster Forks. 1902–03
Silver, each: 7⅝ × ⅝ × ¼"
(19.4 × 1.6 × .6 cm). Manufacturer:
Theodore Müller, Belgium/Germany.
Marshall Cogan Purchase Fund

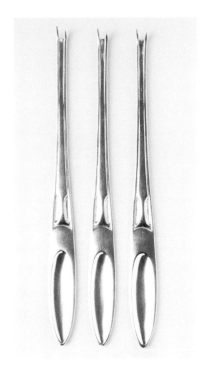

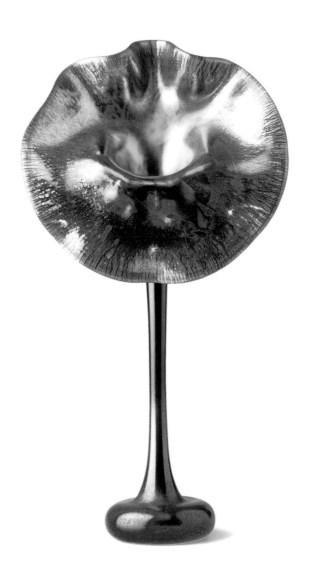

Louis Comfort Tiffany
Vase. 1913
Favrile glass, 20½ × 11 × 4½" (52.1 ×
27.9 × 11.4 cm). Gift of Joseph H. Heil

This vase, often called the Jack-in-the-Pulpit because of its resemblance to the flower bearing that name, is typical of the Art Nouveau style. The slender, elongated neck rising from the bulbous base flares flamboyantly into an undulating rim radiating iridescent violet, blue, and gold. Small veinlike fissures in the finish enhance the organic fluid character of the vase, whose dazzling lustrous surfaces and rich varied colors are hallmarks of Louis Comfort Tiffany, foremost among glassmakers producing opalescent glass at the same time. Working with a staff of chemists and glassblowers, Tiffany developed innovative techniques and methods, moving beyond figurative plant designs applied to traditional forms, toward vessels like this vase, where the form itself evokes the source of inspiration.

Tiffany was the son of the prominent jeweler and silversmith Charles Lewis Tiffany, founder of Tiffany & Co. in New York. Originally trained as a painter in 1879, he first pursued a career in interior design, with commissions for Mark Twain's home and the White House, among others. He founded the Tiffany Glass and Decorating Company on Long Island in 1893, when he began to produce a range of blown-glass vessels he called *favrile*, from the old English word *febrile*, meaning handmade. Tiffany broadened his commercial activities to include metalwork, pottery, enamelware, and jewelry, all of which enjoyed international acclaim, making him one of the first American designers celebrated abroad. —C.L.

Hector Guimard
Entrance Gate to Paris Subway
Station. c. 1900
Painted cast iron, glazed lava, and
glass, 13' 11" × 17' 10" × 32" (424.2 ×
543.6 × 81.3 cm). Gift of Régie
Autonome des Transports Parisiens

The sinuous, organic lines of Hector Guimard's Paris Subway Station design and the stylized, giant stalks drooping under the weight of what seem to be swollen tropical flowers, but are actually amber glass lamps, make this a quintessentially Art Nouveau piece. His designs for this famous entrance arch and two others were intended to visually enhance the experience of underground travel on the new subway system for Paris.

Paris was not the first city to implement an underground system (London already had one), but the approaching Paris Exposition of 1900 accelerated the need for an efficient and attractive means of mass transportation. Although Guimard never formally entered the competition for the design of the system's entrance gates that had been launched by the Compagnie du Métropolitain in 1898, he won

the commission with his avant-garde schemes, all using standardized cast-iron components to facilitate manufacture, transport, and assembly. Parisians were at first hesitant in their response to Guimard's use of an unfamiliar vocabulary, but his Métro gates, installed throughout the city, effectively brought the Art Nouveau style, formerly associated with the luxury market, into the realm of popular culture. —L.L.

Louis Majorelle and Daum Frères
Table Lamp. c. 1900
Gilt and patinated bronze and acid-
etched glass, 27¼ × 11½ × 11½"
(69.2 × 29.2 × 29.2 cm). Joseph H. Heil
Bequest (by exchange)

Hector Guimard
Side Table. c. 1904–07
Pear wood, 29⅞ × 20½ × 17⅞"
(75.9 × 52.1 × 45.4 cm). Gift of
Madame Hector Guimard

Hector Guimard explained his aesthetic inspiration and intentions in nearly cosmic terms: "When I design a piece of furniture or sculpt it, I reflect upon the spectacle the universe provides. Beauty appears to us in perpetual variety. No parallelism or symmetry: forms are engendered from movements which are never alike . . . These dominant lines which describe space, sometimes supple and sinuous arabesques, sometimes flourishes as vivid as the firing of a thunderbolt, these lines have a value of feeling and expression more eloquent than the vertical, horizontal and regular lines continually used until now in architecture."

The inspiration Guimard drew from nature is fully apparent in this Side Table, which was among the furnishings in his own residence and similar to a table he designed for the Hôtel Nozal. There are no right angles. Its sinuous irregular form makes us fully aware of the artist's expressive hand. The biomorphic legs suggest femurs and other skeletal forms, and are simultaneously evocative of plant and animal life, but the inherent abstraction prevents a literal interpretation. The overall contours swell with life, and the carved lines suggest musculature or tendons—lines of force that are resolved at the joints by knuckle-like flourishes.

The Side Table asserts an exuberant and highly individualized vision, and celebrates a modern sensibility that was predicated on the expressive power of the artist to communicate empathically. In retreat from quotidian reality and historic precedent, Guimard effectively modernized design in formal terms as well as expressive content by offering an exploration of psychological sensations and emotions. —P.R.

129

Alvar Aalto
Vase (no. 3031). 1936
Mold-blown glass, 11½ ×
12¼ × 11¼" (29.2 × 31.1 ×
28.6 cm) (irreg.).
Manufacturer: Iittala
Glassworks, Finland
(1954–55). Clarissa
Bronfman Purchase Fund

Alvar Aalto
Paimio Chair. 1931–32
Bent plywood, bent laminated birch,
and solid birch, 26 × 23¾ × 34¾"
(66 × 60.3 × 88.3 cm). Manufacturer:
Oy Huonekalu-ja Rakennustyötehdas
Ab, Finland. Gift of Edgar Kaufmann, Jr.

Admired as much for its sculptural
presence as for its comfort, the
Paimio Chair is a tour de force in
bentwood that seems to test the limits of plywood manufacturing. The
chair's framework consists of two
closed loops of laminated wood,
forming arms, legs, and floor run-
ners, between which rides the
seat—a thin sheet of plywood tightly
bent at both top and bottom into
sinuous scrolls, giving it greater
resiliency. Inspired by Marcel
Breuer's tubular-steel Wassily Chair
of 1927–28, Aalto chose, instead,
native birch for its natural feel and
insulating properties, and developed
a more organic form.
    The Paimio Chair, the best-known
piece of furniture designed by Aalto,
is named for the town in southwest-
ern Finland for which Aalto designed
a tuberculosis sanatorium and all its
furnishings. The angle of the back of
this armchair, which was used in the
patients' lounge, was intended to
help sitters breathe more easily.
    Aalto's bentwood furniture had a
great influence on the American
designers Charles and Ray Eames
and the Finnish-born Eero Saarinen.
In 1935 Artek was established in
Finland to mass-produce and distribute wood furniture designed by Aalto
and his wife, Aino. Most of their
designs remain in production. —P.R.

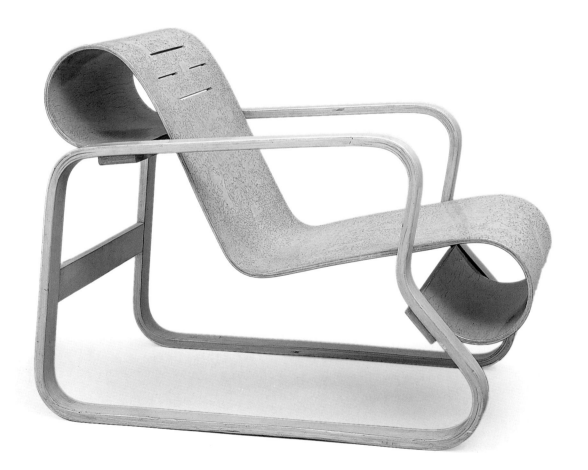

Isamu Noguchi
Table (IN-50). 1944
Ebonized birch and glass,
15⅝ × 50 × 36" (39.7 × 127 × 91.4 cm).
Manufacturer: Herman Miller, Inc.,
USA. Gift of Robert Gruen

"Everything is sculpture," said the designer Isamu Noguchi. Primarily known for his sculpture, he also designed playgrounds, gardens, stage sets, and interiors as well as design objects. His furniture originated from his interest in incorporating sculpture into everyday life and his IN-50 organic freeform coffee table, designed in 1944, is part design and part sculpture: it defines the meeting of organicism and abstraction.

Functionalist in conception and engineering, the piece is simple in design and made for mass production. It is composed of two identically shaped pieces of wood, placed in opposition to one another and joined at a single point by a pin; this ingenious coupling creates a tripod support for an organically shaped glass tabletop. Assembly is so easy that the manufacturer, Herman Miller, originally marketed it as knockdown furniture, shipped in parts and assembled on location. The piece was available with different wood bases: tawny walnut veneer on walnut, Prima Vera veneer on solid birch, and ebonized on solid birch, or with standard lacquer finishes on birch.

Earlier, in 1939, Noguchi had designed a more elaborate version of this table for the president of The Museum of Modern Art, A. Conger Goodyear. The following year, he designed a similar, smaller, and simpler model for the British interior and furniture designer Terence Harold Robsjohn-Gibbings. Noguchi claimed that Robsjohn-Gibbings slightly altered his design and offered it as his own in 1942. Disturbed by this, Noguchi created a similar third table, the IN-50, which was used to illustrate a 1944 article by George Nelson titled "How to Make a Table." Despite the popularity of a number of his industrial designs, Noguchi regarded this coffee table as his only wholly successful furniture design. —B.C.

Frederick Kiesler
Multi-use Rocker. 1942
Prototype: oak and linoleum,
29 × 15¾ × 32¾" (73.7 × 40 × 83.2 cm).
Edgar Kaufmann, Jr. Purchase Fund

Frederick Kiesler
Nesting Coffee Table. 1935–38
Cast aluminum, 9½ × 34 × 25"
(24.1 × 86.4 × 63.5 cm); 9½ × 22 × 16¼"
(24 × 55.9 × 41.3 cm). (1938). Gift of
Carlo M. Grossman and Josie G.
Lindau in memory of their parents
Isobel and Isidore Grossman

Charles and Ray Eames
Lounge Chair. c. 1944
Prototype: molded plywood and steel
rod, 28¾ × 30⅛ × 30" (73 × 76.5 ×
76.2 cm). Gift of the designers

Charles and Ray Eames
Full-Scale Model of Chaise Longue
(La Chaise). 1948
Hard rubber foam, plastic, wood,
and metal, 32½ × 59 × 34¼"
(82.5 × 149.8 × 87 cm). Gift of the
designers

"The form of this chair does not pretend to clearly anticipate the variety of needs it is to fill. These needs are as yet indefinite and the solution of the form is to a large degree intuitive. The form can only suggest a freer adaptation of material to need and stimulate inquiry into what these needs may be."
So read Charles and Ray Eames's description for the design of La Chaise, submitted to The Museum of Modern Art's 1948 International Competition for Low-Cost Furniture Design. The competition, organized by Edgar Kaufmann, Jr., was inspired by the urgent postwar need for low-cost housing and adaptable furnishings for the booming middle class. Coupling designers with manufacturers, the competition produced prototypes eventually exhibited in 1950. They were, in Kaufmann's words, "to be given every chance to reach the general public."

La Chaise was intended to be cheap, lightweight, versatile, and appealing to young families. Its prototype was made from fiberglass—two shells glued together, separated by a rubber disk and filled with styrene. Yet unlike their armchair of the same year, whose prototypes were made from fiberglass but had originally been meant to be stamped out of metal (like the mass-produced automobile)—La Chaise was always intended to be manufactured in fiberglass and retail for $27.00 in 1948. Named for the flowing, rotund, and voluptuous forms of Gaston Lachaise's 1927 sculpture *Reclining Nude*, La Chaise paradoxically denies any sense of mass. Although it proved to be too expensive to manufacture in 1948, La Chaise finally went into production in 1990. —T.d.C.

Tapio Wirkkala
Jäkälä Vase. 1950
Crystal, 3½ × 3½" (8.9 x 8.9 cm) diam.
Manufacturer: Iittala Glassworks,
Finland (1956). Gift of the Finnish
Ministry of Commerce and Industry

Eva Zeisel
Town and Country Salt and Pepper
Shakers. c. 1945
Glazed earthenware, 4½ × 3"
(11.4 × 7.6 cm) diam. Manufacturer:
Red Wing Pottery, USA (1946). Gift of
Della Rothermel in honor of John
Petrick Rothermel

Poul Henningsen
PH Artichoke Lamp. 1958
Copper and steel, 28⅜ × 33¼"
(72.1 × 84.5 cm) diam. Manufacturer:
Louis Poulsen & Co., Denmark (1999).
Gift of the manufacturer

Timo Sarpaneva
Devil's Churn Object. 1951
Glass, 2⅜ × 2⅞" (6 × 7.3 cm) diam.
Manufacturer: Iittala Glassworks,
Finland. Gift of Mr. and Mrs. Albert
Greene

Tapio Wirkkala
Platter. 1951
Plywood, 9⅞ × 1" (25.1 × 2.5 cm).
Gift of Greta Daniel

Sori Yanagi
Butterfly Stool. 1956
Plywood and metal, 15½ × 17⅜ × 12⅛"
(38.4 × 44.1 × 30.8 cm). Manufacturer:
Tendo Co., Ltd., Japan. Gift of the
designer

Strikingly simple in its construction, Sori Yanagi's Butterfly Stool consists of two identical molded plywood pieces held together with a simple brass stretcher and two screws under the seat, which seems to float over the rising curved legs, creating an allusion to the wings of a butterfly in flight. As a type, the stool belongs to the Western interior and has no precedent in Japanese domestic design; yet Yanagi's stool fuses Eastern aesthetics and traditions with the Western influence of postwar occupied Japan. The form of the Butterfly Stool is nevertheless deci-sively Japanese, recalling both architecture, particularly the torii (portals) of Shinto shrines, and calligraphy. Yanagi adopted the use of molded plywood from the pioneering work of the American designers Charles and Ray Eames.

After studying architecture and painting at the Tokyo Academy of Fine Art in 1936–40 Yanagi worked for a time in the architectural office of Junzo Sakakura. Then he served as Charlotte Perriand's assistant in Japan in 1940–42, but never adopted the International Style of modernism, of which Perriand was a practitioner. Instead, his characteristic organic shapes reflected his preference for "gentle and rounded forms [that] radiate human warmth." In 1952, a year after the Allied Forces ended their occupation of Japan, Yanagi opened his own office in Tokyo and the following year was a founding member of the Japan Industrial Designers Association (JIDA) and the Japan Design Committee. He is considered a pioneer of Japanese industrial design and has created a wide range of products, including ceramics, wood furniture, metal tableware, appliances, and lighting. —B.C.

Grete Jalk
Lounge Chair. 1963
Teak, 29½ × 24¾ × 27¼" (74.9 ×
62.9 × 69.2 cm). Manufacturer:
Poul Jeppesen, Denmark. Gift of
Jo Carole and Ronald S. Lauder

Arne Jacobsen
Stacking Side Chair. 1951
Molded plywood, chrome-plated tubular steel, and rubber, 30 × 20½ × 21" (76.2 × 52.1 × 53.3 cm). Manufacturer: Fritz Hansen, Denmark (1952). Gift of Richards Morgenthau Co.

Arne Jacobsen's side chair is popularly known as the "ant" for its insect-thin steel legs, hourglass-profile, and black-lacquer seat and back. This enormously successful chair celebrates an aesthetic minimalism in an industrially produced chair for everyday use. The chair is reduced to two principle parts: the seat and back formed of a single piece of thin molded plywood and a lightweight three-leg tubular-steel frame, to which it is attached with a single joint. Three rubber washers under the seat provide additional stability.

Jacobsen originally designed the chair for the cafeteria of Novo Industry, a pharmaceutical company in Copenhagen. Soon thereafter, it was introduced to a wider market and offered in four different kinds of plywood and black lacquer. The "ant" was Jacobsen's first chair in molded wood laminate, no doubt inspired by the Eames side chairs of the 1940s. Jacobsen's success inspired him to design many subsequent variations with similarly evocative profiles.

The Museum included this chair in the Good Design exhibition of 1955 and acquired it in the same year. After Jacobsen's death, the chair was also produced in a four-leg version and a wide variety of colors. Its popularity has never waned, and more than five million have been produced. —P.R.

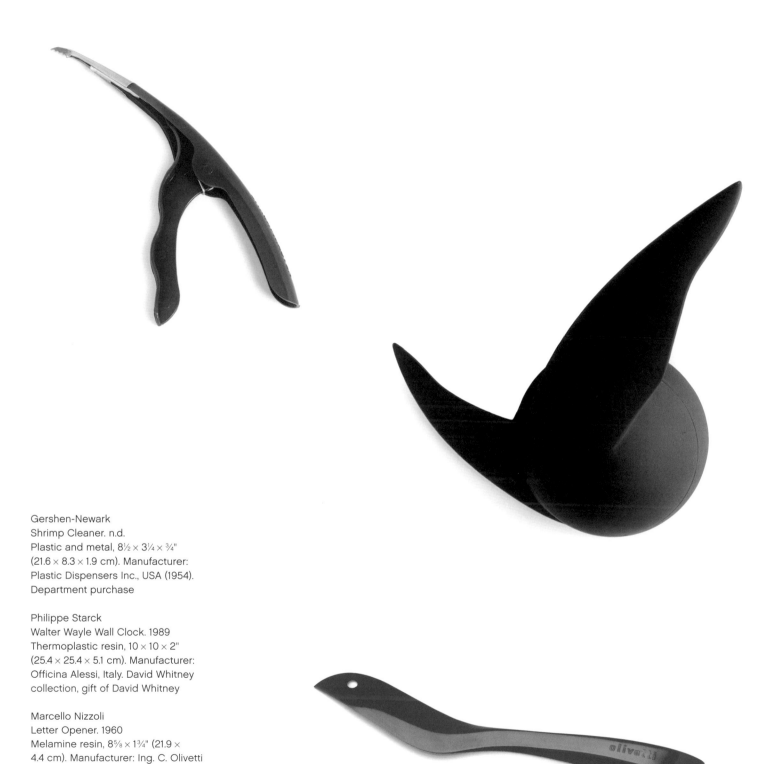

Gershen-Newark
Shrimp Cleaner. n.d.
Plastic and metal, 8½ × 3¼ × ¾"
(21.6 × 8.3 × 1.9 cm). Manufacturer:
Plastic Dispensers Inc., USA (1954).
Department purchase

Philippe Starck
Walter Wayle Wall Clock. 1989
Thermoplastic resin, 10 × 10 × 2"
(25.4 × 25.4 × 5.1 cm). Manufacturer:
Officina Alessi, Italy. David Whitney
collection, gift of David Whitney

Marcello Nizzoli
Letter Opener. 1960
Melamine resin, 8⅝ × 1¾" (21.9 ×
4.4 cm). Manufacturer: Ing. C. Olivetti
& C., Italy. Gift of the manufacturer

Designer unknown
Wine Bottle Stand. Before 1960
Silver-plated metal and raffia,
8¼ × 3¹¹⁄₁₆ × 7½" (21 × 9.4 × 19.1 cm).
Manufacturer: German. Gift of Mark
Cross Co.

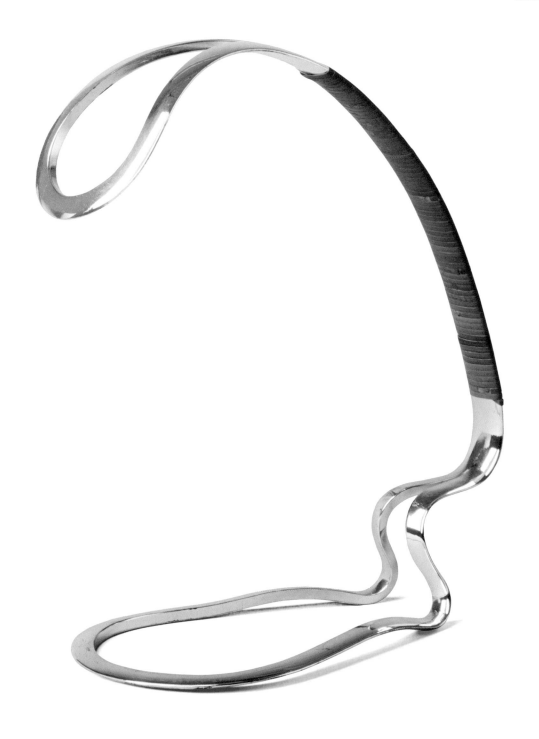

Barbara Ambrosz
Liquid Skin Drinking Cup. 1998
Mouthblown glass, 2 × 5⅛ × 4⅛"
(5.1 × 13 × 10.5 cm). Manufacturer:
Glasatelier Steinschoenau, Austria
(2001). Gift of the manufacturer

Reiko Sudo
Feather Flurries Fabric (no. 9-166A).
c. 1993
Polyester with feathers, 78⅜ × 46⅜"
(199 × 117.8 cm). Manufacturer: NUNO
Corporation, Japan. Gift of the
manufacturer

Marc Newson
Wood Chair. 1988
Wood, 24⅜ × 32¼ × 39¾"
(61.9 × 82.6 × 101 cm). Manufacturer:
Cappellini, Italy. Gift of the
manufacturer

Tom Dixon
S Chair. 1991
Rush and steel, 40⅜ × 19¼ × 22⅞"
(102.6 × 48.9 × 58.1 cm). Manufacturer:
Cappellini, Italy (1997). Gift of the
manufacturer

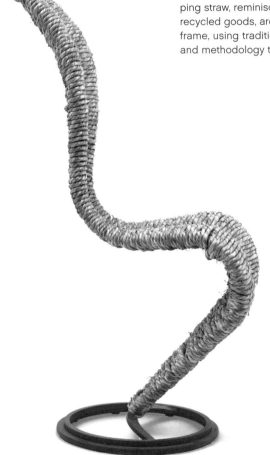

Tom Dixon became a designer after a motorcycle accident when, repairing his bike, he started welding. Soon he began to sell scrap-metal assemblages to his friends. In 1992, he opened the shop Space, in London, to sell his and other artists' work. Two years later, he founded the manufacturer Eurolounge, and in 1998 accepted the position of head of design at the retail chain Habitat.

For his S Chair, Dixon began wrapping straw, reminiscent of found or recycled goods, around a metal frame, using traditional materials and methodology to create a single continuous form that is highly original and contemporary in design. The chair, changing in shape from every angle, suggests a wide variety of organic forms, a leaf, a gourd, a seated figure, or a thin line, meandering like a stream. The cantilever recalls the first tubular-metal chairs of the late 1920s by the Bauhaus modernists Marcel Breuer and Ludwig Mies van der Rohe, while the sinuous form traces the outline of Verner Panton's famous Side Chair of 1960.

Dixon's work has added greatly to the cultural renaissance in Great Britain in the 1990s. His innovative work has coincided deftly with Prime Minister Tony Blair's drive to improve the national design image and compete with other countries. Blair's collaborators coined the somewhat undistinguished slogan Cool Britannia to celebrate England's stature not only in art and architecture—with the Turner Prize, the Millennium dome, Herzog and de Meuron's Tate Modern, and several other high-profile projects—but also in design. The new London-based %100 Design Fair and the presence in town of some of the most admired designers in the world, such as Marc Newson, Ron Arad, and Ross Lovegrove are evidence of this effort. —B.C.

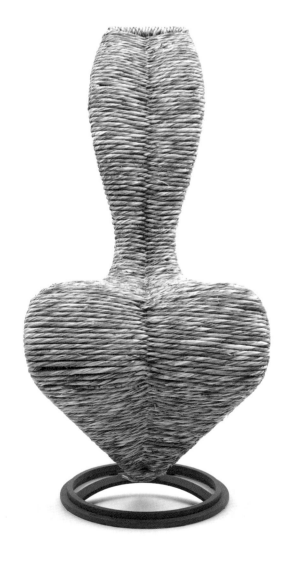

Philippe Starck
W.W. Stool. 1990
Varnished sand-cast aluminum,
38½ × 21¼ × 22⅝" (97.8 × 54 × 57.5 cm).
Manufacturer: Vitra AG, Germany
(c. 1992–2000). David Whitney
collection, gift of David Whitney

Philippe Starck sketched the W.W. Stool as part of a fanciful office environment for the film director Wim Wenders in 1990. The sinuous lines of the sand-cast aluminum, varnished in a pale green, suggest a sprouting plant or even an alien life form. Three roots slither into the floor, with a branch in the front that serves as a footrest. The seed becomes a seat where the shoot winds upward to create a handle for standing support. More a surrealist sculpture than a stool, Starck's design emphasizes form over function. This strangely vital stool incited Philip Johnson to remark: "It's hard to sit on, but extremely inviting sexually."

Psychosexual provocations, sci-fi allusions, and biomorphic forms mingle freely throughout Starck's work. A self-described autodidact, Starck founded his first company for inflatable furniture at the age of nineteen, before he attended the École Centrale des Arts Décoratifs in Paris. In the late 1970s and early 1980s, Starck was celebrated for his interiors of nightclubs and cafés, including the famous Bains-Douches (1978) and Café Costes (1984) in Paris. His career enjoyed a substantial boost in 1982 when the president of France, François Mitterand, commissioned him to design the private chambers in the Elysée palace. Since then, Starck has become a design superstar, with a production ranging from toothbrushes to televisions, from furniture to foodstuffs. Starck is, nonetheless, renowned not only for his prolific industrial production but also for his eclectic interiors for Ian Schrager Hotels, Alain Mikli, Jean-Paul Gaultier, and Hugo Boss. —C.L.

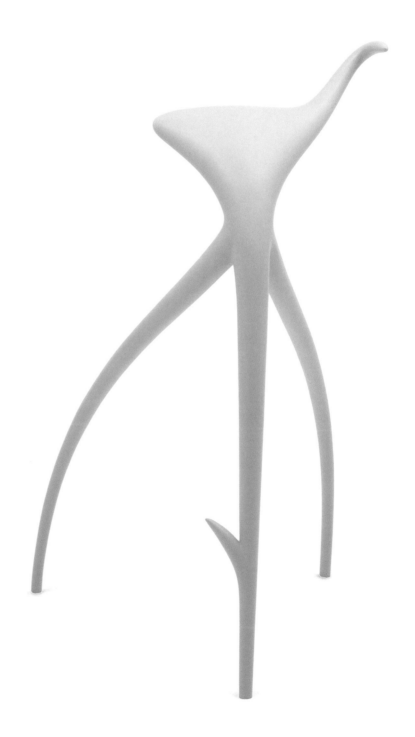

Toshiyuki Kita
The Multilingual Chair. 1991
Fiberglass and steel, 52 × 23⅝ × 23⅝"
(132.1 × 60 × 60 cm). Manufacturer:
Kotobuki Corporation, Japan (1992).
Gift of the manufacturer

Mazda Motor Corp.
MX5 Miata Automobile Taillight. 1983
Acrylic resin, polypropylene plastic,
and other materials, 6¼ × 15 × 4"
(15.9 × 38.1 × 10.2 cm). Gift of the
manufacturer

Claudy Jongstra
SO 070. 2001
Merino wool and silk organza,
85 × 113½" (215.9 × 288.3 cm).
Manufacturer: Not tom dick & harry,
the Netherlands. Frederieke Taylor
Purchase Fund

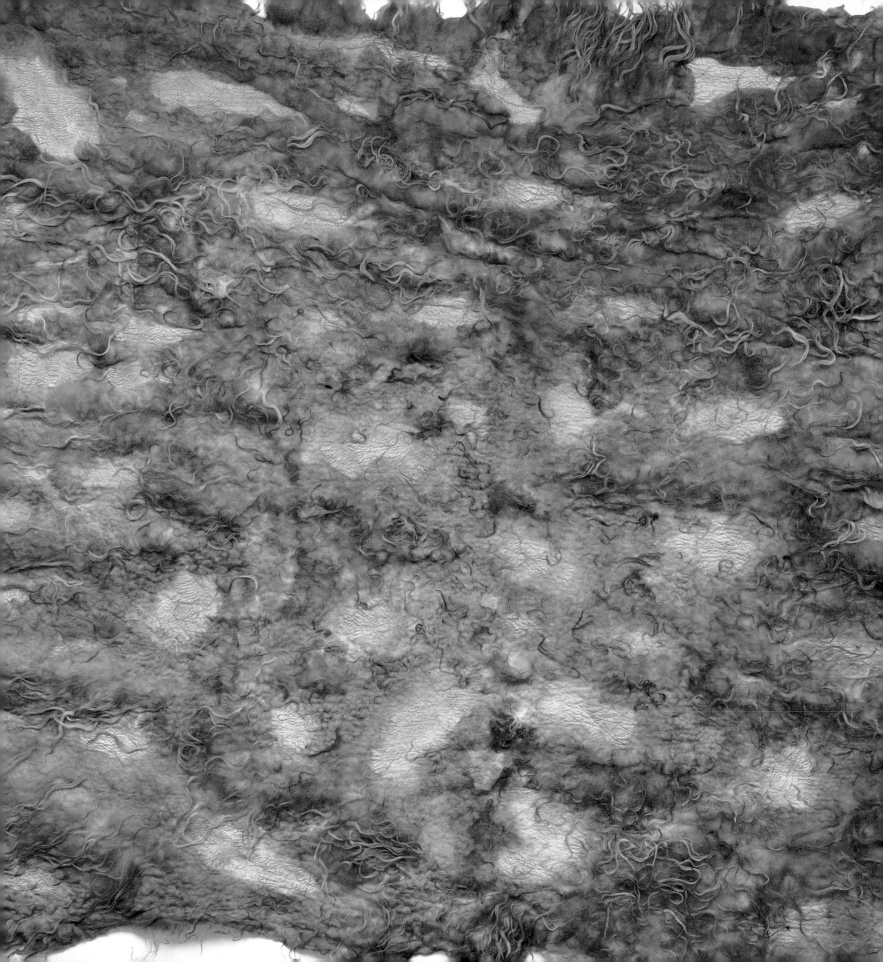

New technologies and materials can provide a designer with astonishing artistic freedom, but as Charles Eames once explained: "As with any tool, the concept and direction must come from the man." The creative mind rarely settles for how it was done before. In the twentieth century, designers were presented with an extraordinary new material world. Never before had there been such widespread innovation. Many of the objects illustrated in this section are made of materials that simply did not exist until the modern age. Improvements continued to be made in the performance of traditional mediums, such as glass, wood, and steel. However, an array of new, mostly synthetic, materials was also invented. Many of these were developed for the defense industry, especially during World War II. When new materials became more widely available, designers explored their aesthetic possibilities and their extraordinary performance, which often led to new functions and applications and astonishingly innovative forms.

Perhaps the single word that best describes the new materials is *plastic*. In the broadest sense, plastic refers to fluid, pliable, and moldable qualities, and, more specifically, it refers to synthetic or natural organic materials, such as resins and polymers, which can be shaped, usually when soft, and hardened. The dream of continuous surfaces without joints has become an inherent reality in the world of plastic materials, resulting in objects with ever more complex curves and profiles, and many that seem impossibly thin.

One of the earliest synthetics was Plexiglas (methyl methacrylate sheet) introduced in 1936 by Rohm & Haas. Among its earliest design applications was Gilbert Rohde's pioneering chair whereby the seat and back, formed of a single sheet of Plexiglas, is attached to steel legs. The novel material's transparent and light qualities that attracted Rohde have continued to fascinate designers, particularly since the performance of acrylics has improved steadily since their invention. Maarten Van Severen's LCP Chaise Longue, available in various colors of transparent polycarbonate, curls like ribbon. The Cone Chair by Fernando and Humberto Campana achieves an elegant transparency with an economy of means and a pedestrian material—polycarbonate.

Developments in plywood technology gave designers the opportunity to form compound curves, bending wood as if it were a new synthetic material. Charles and Ray Eames's Leg Splint, designed in 1942 for injured Navy personnel during the war, pushed the material to its limit of pliability. The experience gained in wartime was applied to their chairs, whose forms had been anticipated in Charles Eames's and Eero Saarinen's prize-winning entry in the Museum's Organic Design in Home Furnishings competition of 1940. When the Eameses turned to fiberglass, the material's performance permitted a chair design whereby the seat, arms, and back are formed from a single shell of polyester, frankly exposed.

New materials, such as polycarbonates and carbon fibers, permitted even thinner and lighter continuous-form objects without joints. Verner Panton's Stacking Side Chair was made by molding polyurethane. The color was integral to the material, which obviated the need to apply color to the surface. The quest to design lightweight furniture was virtually unsurpassed by Alberto Meda's limited-production Light Light Armchair in carbon fiber. A single finger is all that is needed to pick up the chair. Before the invention of carbon fiber (by the defense industry), cast aluminum was prized for its lightness. Hans Coray's Landi Chair with its patterned perforations exemplified lightweight, industrially produced furniture.

Carbon fiber (a graphite material), prized for lightness and strength, has had an enormous impact on the sporting industry because of its ability to enhance performance. Perhaps the most sophisticated example of this is John Barnard's design for Ferrari's Formula 1 Racing Car. The monocoque is a honeycomb of carbon fiber and the synthetic Kevlar—materials originally developed for the aircraft industry that are stronger, stiffer, and lighter than aluminum.

No less compelling are innovations with ordinary materials applied in unexpected ways. Corrugated cardboard, developed in the late nineteenth century as a protective packing material, is an inexpensive, readily available material that Frank Gehry had frequently used for building architectural models. Intrigued by its functional and visual qualities, he produced several collections of furniture, called Easy Edges and Rough Edges, in the 1970s and 1980s respectively, which caused a reconsideration of aesthetic and material values, as well as manufacturing processes. At the time, Gehry considered most furniture to be "ponderous, overpriced, and tyrannical" and instead offered "structural and decorative shapes that were useful, clean, and liberating." Moreover, the furniture was made without sophisticated industrial processes. The social values Gehry associated with cardboard recall the role plastics had played in the 1950s and 1960s, when they represented economy and democracy.

Although the Museum has a long history of exhibiting and collecting innovative design, only recently has it explicitly explored the relationship between "mind and matter," most notably in the 1995 exhibition *Mutant Materials in Contemporary Design*. The exhibition called attention to traditional and new materials applied in unexpected ways, "spawning a new material culture—one that is complex and in a state of continuous change and adaptation." Objects made of ceramics, glass, plastics, composites, metals, and other materials demonstrated their mutable character, the ability "to achieve a different personality." Although many innovations take place in the chemist's laboratory, the exhibition made clear that aesthetic and practical possibilities must come from the designer's mind.

—Peter Reed

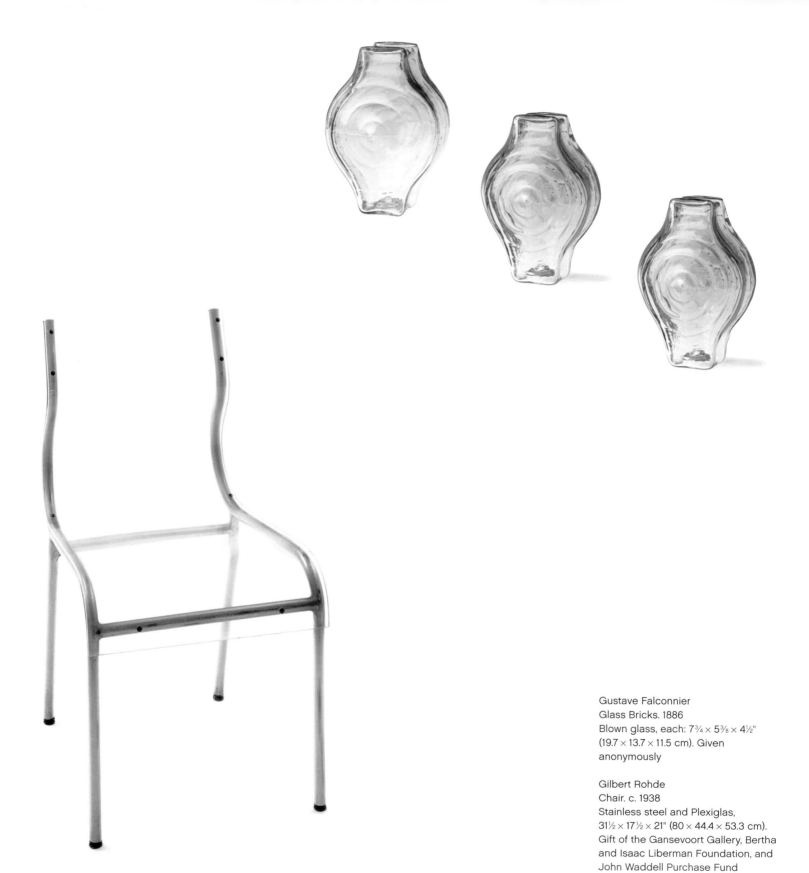

Gustave Falconnier
Glass Bricks. 1886
Blown glass, each: 7¾ × 5⅜ × 4½"
(19.7 × 13.7 × 11.5 cm). Given
anonymously

Gilbert Rohde
Chair. c. 1938
Stainless steel and Plexiglas,
31½ × 17½ × 21" (80 × 44.4 × 53.3 cm).
Gift of the Gansevoort Gallery, Bertha
and Isaac Liberman Foundation, and
John Waddell Purchase Fund

Hans Coray
Landi Chair. 1938
Bent and pressed aluminum
and rubber, 30½ × 21¼ × 22⅛"
(77.5 × 54 × 56.2 cm). Manufacturer:
P. & W. Blattmann Metallwaren-Fabrik,
Switzerland (late 1950s–62). Gift of
Gabrielle and Michael Boyd

Hans Coray's Landi Chair, one of the most successful outdoor chair designs, won a competition to furnish the exhibition grounds of the 1939 Swiss National Exhibition in Zurich. Its name Landi was derived from that of the event in German, Schweizerische Landesausstellung. Some 1,500 were provided for the gardens, squares, and parks; they were made of aluminum, a major Swiss export, highlighted at the fair to represent modern Swiss industry. While aluminum is more expensive than steel, its strength to weight ratio allowed Coray to design a single-shell perforated chair that was exceptionally sturdy and light, weighing only six and a half pounds The chairs stack for storage, and the round openings help reduce the weight as well as prevent the collection of rain or snow.

Using a 300-ton drawing press and technology from the aeronautical industry and the Swiss Federal Railway, Coray created an industrial product with complex curves that could be shaped entirely by machine-pressed aluminum sheet metal with the assistance of Swiss cookware manufacturers. The legs, also machine-pressed, were screwed into place. This design for a molded single-shell chair with a thin splayed-leg frame anticipated the work of Charles and Ray Eames and Eero Saarinen in the 1940s.

The design of the Landi Chair has had only slight alterations since 1939. In the late 1950s, caps were added to the bottoms of the legs, in black or white, to allow their use indoors as well as outside. In 1962, the arrangement of the holes was changed, reducing the number of rows from seven to six, and the number of holes per row from thirteen to ten. From these modifications, we can date the manufacture of the Landi Chair in the Museum's collection to between the late 1950s and 1962. —B.C.

Howard Head
Skis. 1950
Laminated aluminum, plastic,
plywood, and steel edges, each:
77 × 2¾ × ½" (195.6 × 7 × 1.3 cm).
Gift of the manufacturer

Mercedes Franchini
Scooter Sunglasses. 1955
Acrylic plastic and metal,
2½ × 5⅜ × 5½" (6.4 × 13.7 × 14 cm).
Manufacturer: Fopais Franchini, Italy
(1956). Phyllis B. Lambert Fund

Charles and Ray Eames
Leg Splint. 1942
Molded plywood, 4⅛ × 7¾ × 42"
(10.5 × 19.7 × 106.7 cm). Manufacturer:
Evans Products Co., USA (1943–44).
Gift of the designers

Charles and Ray Eames produced, among other things, films, books, architecture, toys, fabrics, interior and exhibition designs, but they are most widely known for their molded plastic and plywood furniture. After they married in 1941, they formed one of the most influential design teams of the twentieth century.

As a result of their interest in bending plywood, they were commissioned by the United States Navy to develop molded wood splints for the legs of injured World War II servicemen because the existing, regulation metal splints amplified the vibrations of the stretcher-bearers and frequently exacerbated injuries. Utilizing their experiments in bending and molding plywood, and inspired by the designs of Ray's wood sculptures, they developed a splint that conformed to the shape of the leg and whose natural material absorbed vibration. The symmetrically placed holes were intended to relieve the stress on the bentwood, and were also used to secure bandages. Approximately 150,000 of these splints were made and used.

The success of the plywood splints led to other commissions using molded plywood, including a nose cone, which is in the Museum's collection, and other parts for a CG-16 glider. The Eameses' work, under contract to the United States Navy and as directors of the Molded Plywood Division of the Evans Products Co. (1943–47), allowed them access to materials derived from industrial processes (plywood, fiberglass, and reinforced plastics), new manufacturing techniques, and funding that otherwise would not have been available. Through this work, they perfected a method of bending, gluing, and molding plywood that ultimately resulted in the designs of their best-known bentwood furniture of 1946. —B.C.

154

Charles and Ray Eames
Rocking Armchair (model RAR).
1948–50
Fiberglass-reinforced polyester, steel,
birch, and rubber shock mounts,
26¾ × 25 × 27⅝" (67.9 × 63.5 × 68.6 cm).
Manufacturer: Herman Miller, Inc.,
USA (1950). Gift of the manufacturer

In 1948, the Museum held an International Competition for Low-Cost Furniture Design, in collaboration with furniture retailers who agreed to manufacture the winning designs. Charles and Ray Eames and their team of designers, in collaboration with members of the engineering department of UCLA, were awarded second prize for their stamped metal chair. Because of the high cost of manufacturing the design in metal, Eames asked the Zenith Plastics company to adapt his design to fiberglass technology, which had been employed to reinforce the plastic radar domes on airplanes during the war. In 1950, when the Museum exhibited the metal chair in the exhibition *Prize Designs for Modern Furniture*, the Herman Miller Furniture Co. contracted with Zenith to begin mass production of the fiberglass version.

It was the first successfully mass-produced molded-plastic chair and was initially offered in three colors with several possible bases, including the Rocking Armchair model with wire struts on birch rockers. Other bases were made with metal rods, wood legs, wire struts, cast-aluminum pedestals, and swivels—all attached to the fiberglass shell with rubber shock mounts. Until 1984, Herman Miller gave the RAR model as a gift to every employee who became a parent. The comfortable contours, tailored to the human body, and simple modern aesthetic made the chairs enormously popular, and inspired many imitations. —C.L.

Bill Stewart
Kodiak Special Bow. n.d.
Laminated wood and fiberglass-
reinforced polyester resin, 61 × 2⅞ ×
2" (154.9 × 7.3 × 5.1 cm). Manufacturer:
Bear Archery Company, USA (1961).
Gift of the manufacturer

Hobie Alter
Expert Model Surfboard. 1958
Balsa, fiberglass, and redwood,
126 × 20" (320 × 50.8 cm). Gift of the
manufacturer

Ernest C. Higgins
Goalie Mask. 1964
Fiberglass, 10½ × 7¾ × 5³⁄₁₆"
(26.7 × 19.7 × 13.2 cm). Emilio
Ambasz Fund

Verner Panton
Stacking Side Chair. 1959–60
Polyurethane plastic, 32⅛ × 19¼ ×
22⅝" (81.6 × 48.9 × 57.3 cm).
Manufacturer: Vitra-Fehlbaum GmbH,
Germany (1968). Gift of Herman Miller
AG, Basel, Switzerland

Verner Panton's Stacking Side Chair marked a watershed in industrial furniture production. It was the first chair cast all in one piece and made entirely from synthetic material. With this chair, Panton pushed polyurethane, a relatively new material with enormous potential, to the limits of what was then technically possible: mass production requiring no assembly or hand labor.

Panton's interest in constructing a chair of a single material may have begun in the early 1950s, while he worked in Arne Jacobsen's studio in Copenhagen. However, Panton attributes his inspiration to having seen firsthand the manufacture of a fiberglass helmet and a plastic bucket. He turned away from the Scandinavian tradition of handcrafted wood furniture to experiment with acrylic and glass fiber-reinforced polyester and foam plastics. Believing, also, that new materials call for new shapes, Panton made his continuous, curving, organic, and somewhat sensuous form, emphasized by a single bright color, accentuate the

malleability and ductility of plastic.

In 1963 Vitra, the licensed producers of the Herman Miller collection, began work on Panton's design. The parent company (and particularly its design director George Nelson) was initially resistant to Panton's chair, claiming: "It is at most a sculpture, but not a chair," in 1967, after much experimentation, the first trial series of 100 to 150 chairs was released. Additional refinements were made, and the final version went into serial production in 1968. —B.C.

Marco Zanuso and Richard Sapper
Lambda Chair. 1959
Painted sheet metal, 30¾ × 15⅜ × 17"
(78.1 × 39 × 43.2 cm). Manufacturer:
Gavina, Italy (1964). Gift of the manu-
facturer

Gino Colombini
Carpet Beater (model KS1475). 1957
Steel-reinforced polyethylene plastic,
23 × 6¼ × 1¼" (58.4 × 15.9 × 3.2 cm).
Manufacturer: Kartell, Italy. Gift of the
manufacturer

Joe Colombo
Stacking Side Chair. 1967
Polypropylene plastic and rubber,
29 × 16½ × 18½" (73.7 × 41.9 × 47 cm).
Manufacturer: Kartell, Italy (1986–87).
Gift of the manufacturer

Joe Colombo
Boby 3 Portable Storage System. 1969
ABS plastic, 29 × 16 × 16⅞" (73.7 ×
40.7 × 42.8 cm). Manufacturer:
Bieffeplast, Italy (1970). Gift of
Inter/Graph

Alberto Meda
Light Light Armchair. c. 1987
Carbon fiber and Nomex composite
honeycomb, 29¼ × 21¾ × 19½"
(74.3 × 55.2 × 49.5 cm). Manufacturer:
Alias, Italy. Gift of the manufacturer

According to Alberto Meda:
"Technology and new materials are
a large warehouse of creative suggestions, which, when looked at with
interpretive ability, go beyond their
strictly technical performance." Meda,
who has a very solid background as
a mechanical engineer, started his
career in the 1970s as the technical
director of Kartell, the plastics manufacturing company. There he began to
forge a unique relationship between
technology and design experimentation, incorporating poetry as well as
engineering into his imaginative solutions. Subsequently, he opened his
own office in Milan.
    Meda has also stated: "Paradox: the
more complex the technology, the
more it is suitable for the production
of objects for simple use, with a uni-
tary image, almost organic." He
demonstrated this idea well with the
Light Light Armchair, his first carbon-
fiber chair, manufactured in a small
series by Alias in 1987. The chair, which
weighs a mere four pounds, is not
only a physical, but also a psychological, representation of lightness. In fact,
user tests conducted with the first
prototypes showed that the chair,
although sturdy, was too lightweight
and too high-tech in appearance for
acceptance by a wide public.
    Often new materials may at first
appear to have surpassed our needs,
as computers seem to have outgrown
the speed of our thoughts and our
fingers. Such profound lifestyle
changes do not occur overnight, but
they do need to start somewhere and
someone has to initiate the process.
Meda is one of the initiators. The
Museum's collection features several
other Meda designs, all of which use
technology to achieve fluidity and
unity of shape and structure. As a
group, Meda's designs represent a
breakthrough in the complex mar-
riage of advanced technology and
objects of everyday use. —P.A.

Stephen Armellino
Bullet-Resistant Mask. 1983
Kevlar and polyester resin,
11 × 6¾ × 3¾" (28 × 17.1 × 9.5 cm).
Manufacturer: U.S. Armor Corporation,
USA. Gift of the manufacturer

Frank O. Gehry
Bubbles Chaise Longue. 1987
Corrugated cardboard with fire-retardant coating, 27¾ × 29 × 76⅜"
(70.5 × 73.7 × 194 cm). Manufacturer: New City Editions, USA. Kenneth Walker Fund

Frank O. Gehry worked with an unexpected, throwaway material—corrugated cardboard—in two series of surprisingly sturdy and humorous home furnishings. The instant success of the first series, Easy Edges, introduced in 1972, earned him international recognition. Gehry conceived its cardboard tables, chairs, bed frames, rocking chairs, and other items to suit the homes of young as well as old, of urban sophisticates as well as country dwellers. The Bubbles Chaise Longue belongs to Experimental Edges, the second series, which was introduced in 1979. These objects were intended to be artworks; yet they are sturdy enough for regular use. As the cardboard wears, it begins to appear suedelike

and soft. Gehry's material lends itself to the curving form of this chair; its rollicking folds are, perhaps, a play on the corrugations themselves.

Heavily marketed and intentionally inexpensive, this furniture epitomized Gehry's interest in promoting affordable good design. The choice of "lowbrow" cardboard for Bubbles reflects Gehry's broad interest in using industrial, commercial, and utilitarian materials. An award-winning architect, he has worked with exposed chain-link fencing, corrugated metal, and plywood in concurrent architectural projects. In both the furniture series and the buildings, Gehry has given value to seemingly worthless materials by using them to create lasting designs. —B.C.

Kyoko Kumai
Wind from the Cloud Wall Hanging. 1992
Stainless steel, 87½ × 115 × 4"
(222.3 × 292.1 × 10.2 cm).
Gift of the designer

Donald T. Chadwick and William Stumpf
Aeron Office Chair. 1992
Glass-reinforced polyester, die-cast aluminum, Hytrel, polyester, and Lycra fibers, 43½ × 27 × 19" (110.5 × 68.6 × 48.3 cm). Manufacturer: Herman Miller, Inc., USA (1994). Gift of the employees of Herman Miller

The design of office chairs requires strict collaboration between designers and engineers and has commanded decades of in-depth research. In the 1960s and 1970s, such designers as Henry Dreyfuss and Niels Diffrient pioneered, in their groundbreaking ergonomic studies, what later became the official parameters of comfort: "When seated and virtually immobile for long periods, the effect can be manifold. The sitting posture causes the abdominal muscles to slacken, curves the spine and impairs the function of some internal organs . . . It is not just the sitting posture but the lack of corrective movement which leads to chronic ailments . . . A well-designed chair does not confine the seated person to any one posture."

In the past thirty years, tremendous progress has been made in this field, resulting in comfortable seats and backs, accessories such as footrests, hand rests, and lumbar supports, new and better fabrics, and enhanced adaptability. The unusual and forceful appearance of most ergonomic chairs, however, has taken some adjustment on the part of office workers. The acquisition of the Aeron chair in 1995 at The Museum of Modern Art sparked a lively and fruitful debate within the Museum. Not only did the chair come with a hefty instruction manual on the operation of its levers and pulleys, but its novel appearance was upsetting to many: it looked like a giant black insect out of a science-fiction movie. Its see-through seat and back looked like wings, while the mechanical box under the seat resembled its digestive organs. Together with some of Frank O. Gehry's buildings and Pedro Almodóvar's movies, it contributed to a re-examination of centuries-old ideas of classical beauty—and of decades-old ideas of modernist beauty as well. —P.A.

Philippe Starck
Jim Nature Portable Television. 1994
High-density wood and plastic, 14⅝ × 15¹³⁄₁₆ × 15" (37.1 × 40.2 × 38.1 cm). Manufacturer: Thomson Consumer Electonics, France. Gift of the manufacturer and gift of David Whitney

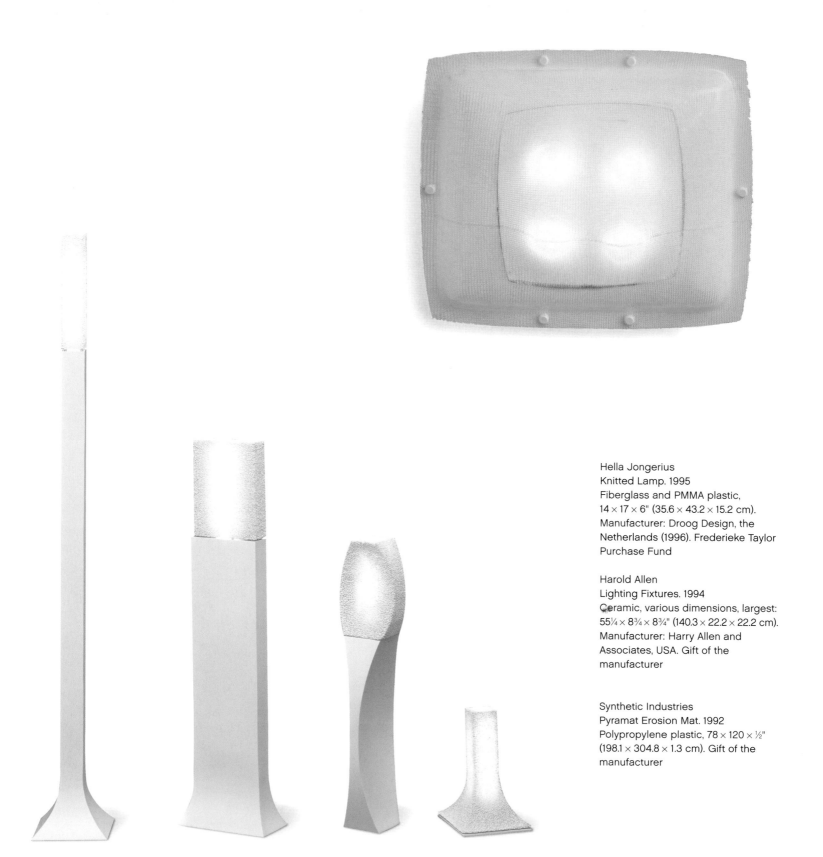

Hella Jongerius
Knitted Lamp. 1995
Fiberglass and PMMA plastic,
14 × 17 × 6" (35.6 × 43.2 × 15.2 cm).
Manufacturer: Droog Design, the
Netherlands (1996). Frederieke Taylor
Purchase Fund

Harold Allen
Lighting Fixtures. 1994
Ceramic, various dimensions, largest:
55¼ × 8¾ × 8¾" (140.3 × 22.2 × 22.2 cm).
Manufacturer: Harry Allen and
Associates, USA. Gift of the
manufacturer

Synthetic Industries
Pyramat Erosion Mat. 1992
Polypropylene plastic, 78 × 120 × ½"
(198.1 × 304.8 × 1.3 cm). Gift of the
manufacturer

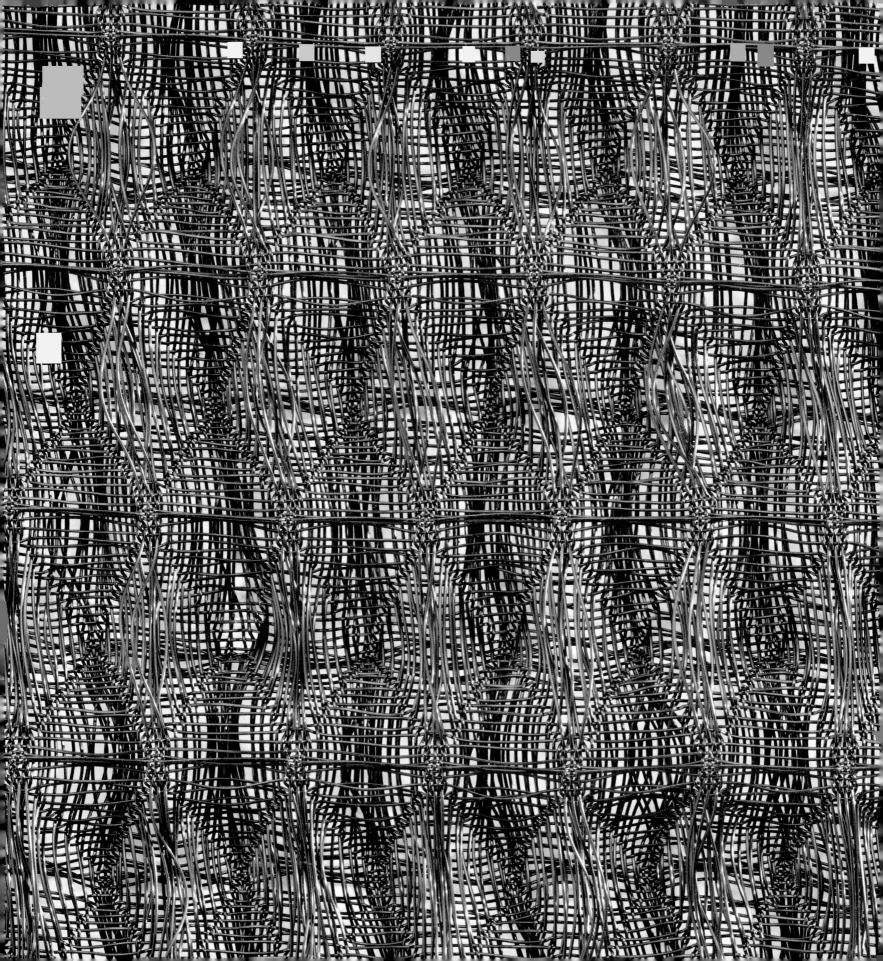

John Barnard and Ferrari S.p.A. Formula 1 Racing Car (641/2). 1990 Honeycomb composite with carbon fibers, Kevlar, and other materials, 40½ × 84 × 176½" (102.9 × 213.4 × 448.3 cm). Gift of the manufacturer

The design of the Formula 1 Racing Car is predicated on a single purpose—to win the high-stakes Grand Prix races. State-of-the-art technology and engineering coupled with the designer's intuitive abilities inform the car's shape. There is nothing superfluous in this sophisticated machine, which has a top speed of 210 miles per hour.

The great challenge was to move the driver at the fastest possible speed without compromising safety. Aerodynamics, as well as wind-tunnel studies and computer calculations influence the car's shape. Airflow is a critical factor—not only to minimize drag and resistance, but also to cool the engine and brakes and help maintain stability. The front and rear wings produce the necessary down-force to keep the car from becoming airborne. The driver's cockpit is fabricated with innovative synthetic materials, originally developed for the aircraft industry, which are stronger, stiffer, and lighter than aluminum, which was more common in earlier cars.

John Barnard was responsible for the overall design of the car, with the exception of the engine itself, which was engineered and designed by Ferrari. When the Formula 1 was first exhibited at the Museum in 1993, Barnard described his process in an interview: "I always try to get to the point where everything has been thought about before we commit to the final shape. I always feel the shape should be very homogenous. Unless there's a really strong reason to have a break in a line . . . then the lines should all be flowing. I think there's an inherent aerodynamic quality to that." —P.R.

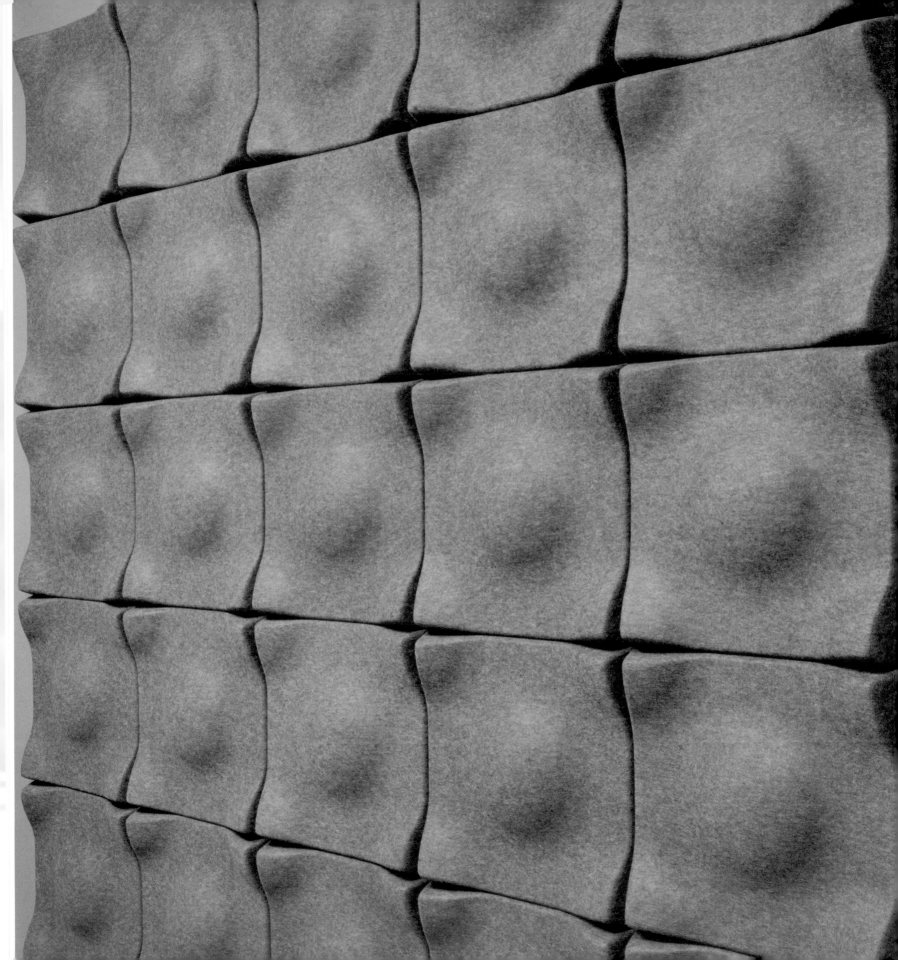

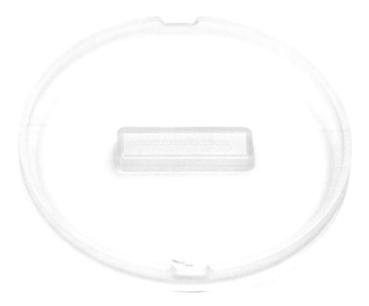

Sam Hecht, Chris Chapman, and
David Sandbach
ElekTek Conference Telephone. 2000
Prototype: injection-molded
methacrylate and ABS, ElekTex,
perforated aluminum, and other
plastic materials, 2½ × 8¼ × 8¼"
(6.4 × 21 × 21 cm). Manufacturer:
Electrotextiles Co. (now ElekSen Ltd.),
England. Gift of the manufacturer

Prototypes for effective design solutions to simplify the way we work were introduced for the first time at the Museum in 2001. Among them was Sam Hecht's ElekTek Conference Telephone, signifying a major change of direction.

The Hecht telephone was designed using a new composite material called ElekTex, which looks and feels like a fabric and can be folded, wrapped, or scrunched, but is in reality a full-fledged intelligent interface, combining a patented conductive fabric sensor and proprietary electronic and software systems. ElekTex can sense via three axes (X, Y, and Z) within a textile-fabric structure approximately 1 mm thick. Its sensing relies on position, pressure, and switch arrangement. The resulting fabric interfaces deliver data according to the product, be it a telephone or a keyboard, and can be applied to many different substrates, from foam to metal.

The international engineering and design firm IDEO, well known for its work in giving form to technical innovation, was called upon to design the very first prototypes. In the past, many designers and students have dreamed of soft or foldable electronic accessories that would be easy to carry and store. Hecht's team in IDEO's London office followed these leads and fully exemplified the possibilities of the material. —P.A.

7 | Good Design

Between 1950 and 1955, the Museum sponsored a series of Good Design exhibitions, intended to influence wholesale buyers, who determined which furnishings appear in stores throughout the country, as well as convince manufacturers of a potentially large market for well-designed objects. The series was held bi-annually at the Chicago Merchandise Mart, America's largest wholesale market, and annually at The Museum of Modern Art. Its aim was educational, insofar as the Museum strove to circulate exhibitions to schools, universities, and department stores; and commercial, as it also aimed to expand the consumer market through a complex strategy of exhibitions, publications, symposia, advertising, and opinion polls. The ultimate goal was to influence and encourage tasteful consumption, through presenting a "balance of retrospect and forecast" and a selection based on "eye-appeal, function, construction, and price, with emphasis on the first."

The series was conceived and organized by Edgar Kaufmann, Jr., the son of a Pittsburgh businessman who had established a prosperous department store. Like many proponents of design at the time, he had no formal training; his acumen and eye as a curator owed much to observation and to first-hand merchandising experience in the home-furnishings department of his father's store. Joining the staff of the Museum in 1946, at the end of the Useful Objects series, Kaufmann envisioned a broad collaboration between art and commerce for his exhibition program. There were precedents for his thinking: his friend Alexander Girard, who later became a designer at Herman Miller, staged an exhibition, *For Modern Living*, at the Detroit Institute of the Arts in 1949, and, in the same year, according to Kaufmann, "Twelve American museums of art . . . held exhibitions of applied art to guide the public toward good taste in objects available for purchase." But the realization of an exhibition of such scale in the United States,

intended to influence the buying habits of the average consumer, was unparalleled. In fact, only the Deutscher Werkbund of 1920, which responded to burgeoning industrialization in its attempts to reform the applied arts by working closely with museums, manufacturers, artist guilds, and retailers, ever rivaled its ambition and scope.

Like the Werkbund's activities, the Good Design series was a response to postwar prosperity, when designers and manufacturers found a common ground in their desire to improve the quality of ordinary life through technology. The series paired the growing middle class and the increasing market for mass-produced furniture for the home of the 1950s, spearheaded by such companies as Herman Miller and Knoll Associates. Herman Miller, founded in 1923 in Zeeland, Michigan, as a small furnishings company, had by the 1950s become a pioneer of contemporary design. Likewise, Knoll Associates rose to prominence when Hans Knoll, a German émigré with a strong knowledge of manufacturing and marketing, married a young gifted designer from the Academy of Art at Cranbrook. Together, they championed the Bauhaus tenets of good design, technological innovation, and mass production.

Kaufmann's criteria for the Good Design products cast a wide net. His emphasis on eye-appeal and the requirement that each object be new apparently linked the new with the good and seemingly valued style over art. Such an intuitive and deductive approach, derived from sentiment and "the progressive taste of the day," differed notably from the inductive principles of beauty and utility put forth by Alfred H. Barr, Jr., Philip Johnson, and John McAndrew. In their essays for *Machine Art*, Barr and Johnson equated good design with modern design, specifically, "good machine art." Implied in Barr's consideration of design objects and fine art was the assumption that objects, like art, should resist falling prey to mere style or fashion and should "distill the eternal from the transi-

tory." Johnson went further, deriding the superficial eye-appeal characteristic of much of American design, touting instead the machine technics of speed, simplicity, precision, smoothness, and reproducibility. "Besides the French Decorative movement in the '20's," he wrote, "there developed in America a desire for 'styling' objects for advertising. Styling a commercial object gives it more eye-appeal and therefore helps sales. Principles such as streamlining often receive homage out of all proportion to their applicability." It was such "styling," especially streamlining, that McAndrew, as the curator of the Useful Objects series, had regarded as the antithesis to good functional design. McAndrew had tied the selection of objects to price, thus linking good design to good value rather than style.

Paradoxically, while Kaufmann was criticized by George Nelson and others for having fallen prey to personal taste and a "non-ideological" approach, his Museum exhibitions included and successfully identified almost every major designer of his time, from Alvar Aalto, Arne Jacobsen, Kaj Franck, Finn Juhl, and Eva Zeisel, to the wave of European émigrés schooled at Cranbrook, including Florence Knoll, Harry Bertoia, Charles and Ray Eames, Alexander Girard, Jack Lenor Larsen, and Eero Saarinen, to name just a few.

Kaufmann's visionary ideas still resonate, at a time when the American market is largely driven by image and branding, and all attempts to bring good design to the household are made by promoting image and prestige attached to celebrity. He attempted to lead the public's eye toward standards of discernment using a set of guiding principles that endures today: that the quality of objects be judged on the basis of form, that prices be suitable to most people's means, that there be an interest in materials and processes of production, and that there exist an overall appreciation of aesthetics.

—Tina di Carlo

Aino Aalto
Tumbler. 1932
Pressed glass, 3⅜ × 3" (8.6 × 7.6 cm)
diam. Manufacturer: Iittala Glassworks,
Finland. Greta Daniel Fund

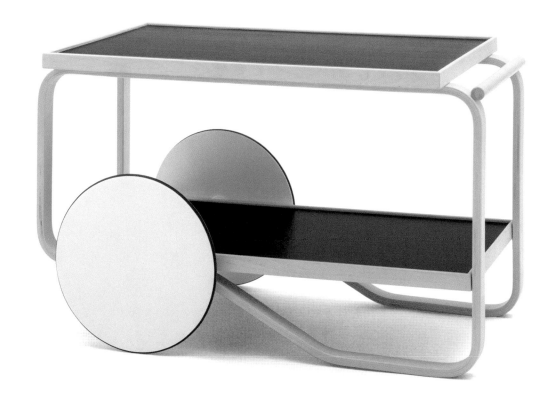

Alvar Aalto
Stacking Stool (model 60). 1932–33
Birch, 17¼ × 13¾" (43.8 × 35 cm) diam.
Manufacturer: Oy Huonekalu-ja
Rakennustyötehdas Ab, Finland.
Phyllis B. Lambert Fund

Alvar Aalto
Tea Trolley (model 98). 1936–37
Linoleum, birch, lacquer, and rubber,
22⅛ × 19¾ × 35½" (56.1 × 50.2 ×
90.2 cm). Manufacturer: Oy
Huonekalu-ja Rakennustyötehdas Ab,
Finland (1980). Gift of ICF, Inc.

Jorge Ferrari Hardoy, Antonio Bonet,
and Juan Kurchan
B.K.F. Chair. 1938
Painted wrought-iron rod and leather,
overall: 34⅜ × 32¾ × 28¾"
(87.3 × 83.2 × 73 cm). Manufacturer:
Artek-Pascoe, USA (c. 1941–43).
Edgar Kaufmann, Jr. Fund

Charles and Ray Eames
Three-Legged Side Chair. c. 1944
Plywood, lacquered metal, rubber
shock mounts, and glides,
30 × 19 × 22½" (76.2 × 48.3 × 57.2 cm).
Manufacturer: Evans Products Co.,
USA (1946). Gift of the manufacturer

190

When Charles and Ray Eames first produced the LCM (Lounge Chair Metal) chair and its companion the DCM (Dining Chair Metal) in 1946 they met with great commercial success. Both had a molded-plywood seat and back that sat on a chrome-plated steel frame with rubber shock mounts in between, and differed principally in height, with the dining chair being two inches taller. That the back and seat are separate pieces simplified production, while also providing visual interest.

Together with Eero Saarinen, Eames had first experimented with bent plywood in 1940 on several prizewinning furniture designs. These, however, proved difficult to manufacture, and most of them were upholstered. Intent on producing high-quality objects at economical manufacturing costs, the Eameses devoted the better part of the next five years to refining the technique of molding plywood to create thin shells with compound curves that offered comfort without upholstery. The first manufacturer of this chair was the Evans Products Co., but in 1949 Herman Miller bought the rights to produce it. —P.A.

Charles and Ray Eames
Low Side Chair (model LCM). 1946
Molded walnut-veneered plywood, chrome-plated steel rods, and rubber shock mounts, 27⅜ × 22¼ × 25⅜" (69.5 × 56.5 × 64.4 cm). Manufacturer: Herman Miller Inc., USA. Gift of the manufacturer

Kaj Franck
Salt and Pepper Shakers. 1947
Glazed earthenware, each: 2⅜ × 1⅝"
(6 × 4.1 cm) diam. Manufacturer:
Wärtsilä-Koncernen AB, Finland
(1952). Skidmore, Owings & Merrill
Design Collection Purchase Fund

Hendrik Van Keppel and Taylor Green
Lounge Chair and Ottoman. 1946
Enameled tubular steel and cotton:
chair 25¾ × 21 × 34⅜" (65.4 × 53.3 ×
87.3 cm); ottoman 12¼ × 21⅜ × 18⅜"
(31.1 × 54.3 × 46.7 cm). Gift of Mr. and
Mrs. Gifford Phillips

Allan Gould
Side Chair. 1952
Steel and plastic cord, 31⅛ × 16³⁄₁₆ ×
17¹³⁄₁₆" (79.1 × 41.1 × 45.2 cm).
Gift of the manufacturer

Gio Ponti
Superleggera Side Chair. 1956
Wood and wicker, 32¾ × 16⅝ × 18¼"
(83.2 × 42.2 × 46.4 cm). Manufacturer:
Cassina, Italy. Gift of the manufacturer

Isamu Noguchi
Rocking Stool. 1954
Chrome-plated steel and walnut,
16½ × 14⅛" (41.9 × 35.9 cm) diam.
Manufacturer: Knoll Associates, USA
(c. 1957). Barbara Jakobson Purchase
Fund

George Nelson
Tray Table (model 4950). 1948
Walnut plywood and steel,
19½ × 15¹³⁄₁₆ × 15¹³⁄₁₆" (49.5 × 38.5 ×
38.5 cm). Manufacturer: Herman
Miller, Inc., USA (1949). Gift of Fifty/50

George Nelson believed that furniture should be "a simple, direct expression of construction with existing techniques." A 1931 graduate of Yale's School of Fine Arts, Nelson became an architect after graduate school (at Catholic University), when building was at a standstill owing to the Great Depression and World War II. The first project for which he gained recognition—his Storage Wall, a flexible system of collapsible parts based on the idea of "thickening the wall" and thereby providing maximum storage with minimal clutter—reinforced his lifelong pursuit of the integration of architecture and furniture. It also landed him the post of director of the Herman Miller furniture company, a position he held from 1946 to 1965. His belief in a market for good, honest design became the trademark of the company as well as his own designs.

The Tray Table demonstrates his characteristic economy of means and form, and his belief in adjustable furniture, which, when disassembled, could be stocked neatly and compactly.

Nelson's tenure at Herman Miller made him one of the most influential figures in modern American design: he commissioned work by Eames, Alexander Girard, and Robert Propst, all of whom made significant contributions to the field. He always favored standardized elements and economical production that increased space, utility, and harmony, but paradoxically left out any mention of popularity when expressing his philosophy. At a Chicago conference, when he was asked why Herman Miller products were prohibitively expensive for the average consumer, he quipped: "As a designer, I don't give a damn about people." —T.d.C.

Charles and Ray Eames
Eames Storage Unit (ESU). 1950
Plastic-coated plywood, lacquered
Masonite, and chrome-plated steel,
58½ × 47 × 16¾" (148.6 × 119.4 × 42.5 cm).
Manufacturer: Herman Miller, Inc.,
USA. Gift of John C. Waddell

Donald R. Knorr
Side Chair. 1948–50
Sheet metal, steel rods, rubber
foam, and fabric, 30½ × 23 × 19"
(77.5 × 58.4 × 48.3 cm). Manufacturer:
Knoll Associates, USA. Gift of the
manufacturer

The Ironrite Ironer Co.
Work Chair. n.d.
Steel and lacquered plywood,
26¼ × 17½ × 19½" (66.7 × 44.5 × 49.5 cm).
Manufacturer: The Ironrite Ironer Co.,
USA (1938). Gift of the manufacturer

Greta Von Nessen
Anywhere Lamp. 1951
Aluminum and enameled metal,
14¾ × 14¼" (37.5 × 36.2 cm) diam.
Architecture and Design Fund

Achille and Pier Giacomo Castiglioni
Luminator Floor Lamp. 1955
Enameled steel and other materials,
72 × 21 × 17½" (182.9 × 53.3 × 44.4 cm).
Manufacturer: Gilardi & Barzaghi, Italy.
Purchase

L. M. Ericsson Telephone Co.
Ericofon Telephones. 1949–54
ABS plastic, rubber, and nylon, each:
9⅛ × 3⅞ × 4⅜" (23.2 × 9.8 × 11.1 cm).
Given anonymously

The Ericofon Telephone combines the earpiece, mouthpiece, dial, and switch in a single compact sculptural form, an innovation made possible by advances in technological miniaturization and lighter materials. The underside features a recessed dial enclosed by a rubber gasket, with a red nylon ball switch at the center that is activated by the weight of the phone. The circuitry is located in the base for balance and stability. The Ericofon was developed by a team of designers, beginning with a series of organic models that studied the efficient arrangement and aggregate weight of the components. The aim was to distribute the elements for ease of use in such a way as not to exceed the weight of the handset of the standard two-piece telephone. In 1956, the Ericofon was introduced in six different colors, in the United States and Europe.

Lars Magnus Ericsson founded the L.M. Ericsson Telephone Co. in 1876, as a telegraph repair shop. Two years later the company began to manufacture telephones. The earliest models were based on Alexander Graham Bell's design, which was followed by many new designs, among them the European cradle desk telephone of 1909 and one of the first plastic telephones designed in 1930. Today, Ericsson has become one of the world's largest producers in the communications industry. —C.L.

Eero Saarinen
Tulip Armchair (model 150). 1955–56
Fiberglass-reinforced polyester and
cast aluminum, 31½ × 25¼ × 23½"
(80 × 64.1 × 59.7 cm). Manufacturer:
Knoll International, Inc., USA (c.
1956–58). Gift of the manufacturer

The Tulip Armchair, which resembles
the flower but also a stemmed wine-
glass, is part of Eero Saarinen's last
furniture series. This one-legged
chair was meant to alleviate one of
Saarinen's great concerns: clutter.
Describing his intentions to simplify
and clarify structure, he said: "The
undercarriage of chairs and tables in
a typical interior makes an ugly, con-
fusing, unrestful world. I wanted to
clear up the slum of legs. I wanted to
make the chair all one thing again."
Saarinen designed each piece in the
Tulip series of furniture with a single
pedestal leg, creating a unified environment of chairs, tables, and stools.
    The Tulip Armchair also marks the
culmination of Saarinen's efforts to
create a chair molded from a single
material, which furthered his design
concept of "one piece, one material."
But, while the elegant chair looks as if
it is made of all one material, the
sculptural fiberglass shell seat is
actually supported on an aluminum
stem with a fused plastic finish. —B.C.

Timo Sarpaneva
Casserole. 1959
Cast iron and teak, 7 × 8 × 7¾"
(17.8 × 20.3 × 19.7 cm). Manufacturer:
W. Rosenlew & Co., Finland. Gift of
the designer

Architetti Montagni, Berizzi, Butte
Phonola Television (model 1718). 1956
Metal and wood, 22 × 19 × 19"
(55.9 × 48.2 × 48.2 cm). Manufacturer:
Phonola, Italy. Given anonymously

Charles and Ray Eames
Lounge Chair and Ottoman. 1956
Molded rosewood, plywood, leather,
cast aluminum, rubber shock mounts,
and stainless steel glides, two parts:
chair 33 × 33¾ × 33" (83.8 × 85.7 ×
83.8 cm); ottoman 16 × 26 × 21"
(40.6 × 66 × 53.3 cm). Manufacturer:
Herman Miller Furniture Co., USA.
Gift of the manufacturer

The Eames Lounge Chair and
Ottoman, with down-filled leather
cushions and a seat that swivels
and tilts, exudes comfort. Charles
and Ray Eames hoped this chair
and ottoman would have the "warm
receptive look of a well-used first
baseman's mitt," a decidedly mas-
culine American metaphor that
seems appropriate. Eames said that
he originally produced the chair as
a present for his friend Billy Wilder,
the legendary filmmaker; but
regardless of its initial impetus, the
chair and ottoman have gained

wide appeal and remain in production. This popular chair, often called
the twentieth-century interpretation
of a nineteenth-century English
club chair, exhibits a softer human-
izing modernism. It was the last
in a long series of plywood-shell
chairs designed by Eames that
began in 1940.

The lounge chair comprises three
double-curved plywood shells with
rosewood veneer and padded
with leather cushions: the headrest,
back, and seat. These elements are
joined together by cast-aluminum

connectors. The chair and the
ottoman are each supported by a
star-shaped metal base on
stainless-steel glides. In addition to
the black leather, the chair was
available in a variety of colors and
materials, including Naugahyde and
fabrics designed by Alexander
Girard. Although some critics considered the chair ugly, awkward, and
too luxurious for popular consumption, it was generally well received,
won the gold medal at the 1960
Milan Triennale, and has become
an emblem of modern design. —P.R.

Max Bill
Wall Clock (model 32/0389). 1957
Chrome-plated metal, 2⅜ × 12¾"
(6 × 32.4 cm) diam. Manufacturer:
Gebrüder Junghans AG, Germany.
Philip Johnson Fund

Bruno Munari
Cubo Ashtray. 1957
Anodized aluminum and melamine
resin, 3¼ × 3¼ × 3¼" (8.3 × 8.3 × 8.3 cm).
Manufacturer: Danese Milano, Italy.
Gift of the manufacturer

Florence Knoll
Coffee Table. 1954
Rosewood and chrome-plated metal,
17 × 27⅛ × 27⅛" (43.2 × 68.9 × 68.9 cm).
Manufacturer: Knoll International, Inc.,
USA (c. 1954–73). Barbara Jakobson
Purchase Fund

Charles and Ray Eames
Lounge Chair and Ottoman. 1958
Polished die-cast aluminum and
fabric, chair: 39¾ × 23 × 30"
(101 × 58.4 × 76.2 cm). Manufacturer:
Herman Miller Furniture Co., USA.
Gift of the manufacturer

Osvaldo Borsani
Armchair (P40). 1955
Wool, polyurethane foam, and steel,
33⅛ × 27¹⁵⁄₁₆ × 46⅛" (84 × 71 × 117 cm).
Manufacturer: Tecno, Italy. Gift of the
manufacturer

Serge Mouille
Floor Lamp. c. 1950
Painted brass and steel,
64³⁄₁₆ × 37 × 37³⁄₁₆" (163 × 94 × 94.4 cm).
Patricia Phelps de Cisneros Purchase
Fund

Luigi Massoni and Carlo Mazzeri
Cocktail Shaker. 1957
Stainless steel, 7⅞ × 3¼" (20 × 8.2 cm)
diam. Manufacturer: Alessi, Italy.
Given anonymously

Arne Jacobsen
Cylinda Ashtray. 1964–67
Stainless steel, 2⁹⁄₁₆ × 2¹⁵⁄₁₆" (6.5 × 7.5 cm)
diam. Manufacturer: Stelton A/S,
Denmark. Gift of Bonniers, Inc.

Magnus Stephensen
Tanaqvil Flatware. 1955
Stainless steel, largest: 13¾ × 2⅛"
(34.9 × 5.4 cm). Manufacturer: Georg
Jensen Sølvsmedie, Denmark.
Gift of the manufacturer

Kaj Franck
Pitcher and Glasses. 1954
Turn-mold blown glass, pitcher:
8¾ × 3⅞" (22.2 × 9.9 cm) diam.
Manufacturer: Nuutajärvi Glass
Works, Finland. Best Products Co.
Fund

A pioneering force in the awakening of Finnish postwar design, Kaj Franck believed that utilitarian wares should first and foremost serve the needs of the user. His objects, designed during a period in Scandinavia when affordable, well designed, highly functional, and mass produced objects flourished, correspond to his belief that a certain truth is embodied in an object that simply and elegantly fulfills its purpose.

The pitcher shown here demonstrates the way in which Franck strove to make his products universal and useful, to attain what he called the "optimal object." Designed to avoid the expensive, time-consuming task of manufacturing a handle and produced in warm hues of red, green, and amber, the pitcher is a cylinder, slimmed at the center in order to be grasped with one hand. Franck saw in pure geometry an absence of socioeconomic connotations and the fluctuations of fashion. Because he was enamored of the indigenous functional craft of Finland—how an ordinary bowl common in rustic homes is an ideal functional object—his designs reflect a humanist attitude, a search for the perfect relationship between man and the mass-produced object.

Franck was trained as an interior designer at the Institute of Industrial Arts, Helsinki, from 1929 to 1932. He began designing objects only in 1945, when he was named artistic director at Arabia, a substantial ceramics manufacturer since 1873. In 1952 he became known for his Kilta series of multipurpose ceramic tableware. It was designed with simple interchangeable colored forms, and was produced from 1953 through 1975 (and since 1981 as the Teema series). —T.d.C.

Ferdinand Porsche and
Volkswagenwerk
Volkswagen Type 1 Sedan. 1938
Steel, 59" × 60½" × 13' 4" (149.9 × 153.7
× 406.4 cm). Acquired with assistance
from Volkswagen of America, Inc.

The most popular automobile in
the world, the Volkswagen Type 1
Sedan, popularly known as the
Beetle, completely transcended its
German roots, and became an international phenomenon in the 1950s.
The Volkswagen sedan has been
remarkable for its formal consistency
since production began in 1938. The
basic shape has undergone relatively few changes in subsequent
models.

The design of the Volkswagen can
be traced to the noted German
automobile designer Ferdinand

Porsche. By the early 1930s, Porsche had developed a prototype for an affordable "people's car" (Volkswagen). His challenge was to create an innovative design that was not simply a scaled-down large car. He explained: "By a people's car, I understand only a completely practical vehicle that can compete with every other practical vehicle on equal terms. In my opinion, a fundamentally new approach is needed to turn normal vehicles, existing hitherto, into people's cars."

Porsche's new approach was based on aerodynamic research and an economical use of steel; in addition, a rear-mounted, air-cooled engine contributed much to the car's success. The bulbous design provided ample headroom in the interior. During the 1930s, Adolf Hitler seized the opportunity to develop the project, but few civilian models were produced before World War II. When Volkswagen was reestablished after the war, the design and engineering of the Volkswagen was modified, but the overall appearance resembled Porsche's original design. In 1959,

the company produced 575,407 sedans to meet a rising international demand. The Museum's "mignonette green" Volkswagen Type 1 Sedan of that year exhibits several features typical of the cars sold in America at the time, such as whitewall tires and "towel-rail" bumpers. The size of the rear window was increased from earlier models to improve visibility. Whereas, in postwar Germany, the Volkswagen was associated with lean and hard times, in America it was associated with fun, economy, youth, and independence. —P.R.

Marco Zanuso and Richard Sapper
Grillo Folding Telephone. 1965
ABS plastic, 2¾ × 6½ × 3¼" (7 × 16.5 × 8.3 cm). Manufacturer: Societá Italiana Telecomunicazioni Siemens, Italy (c. 1967–68). Gift of the manufacturer

Achille and Pier Giacomo Castiglioni
Arco Floor Lamp. 1962
Marble and stainless steel, 8' 2½" ×
6' 7" × 12½" (250 × 200 × 31.75 cm).
Manufacturer: Flos, Italy. Gift of the
manufacturer

Achille Castiglioni has designed more than sixty lamps and a host of other objects, working from 1945 until 1968 with his brother Pier Giacomo and then on his own. One of their best-known lamp designs, Arco, came about through the challenge of a practical problem: how to provide an overhead lamp that would not require drilling a hole in the ceiling.

Castiglioni's motto, "design demands observation," proved accurate, for it was a street lamp that gave the brothers the inspiration for this fixture. Street lamps, affixed to the ground, have a shape that enables them to project their light beams several feet away from their bases. In this domestic adaptation, the Castiglionis were able to illuminate objects eight feet away from the lamp's base—far enough to light the middle of a dining table—by inserting a steel arch into a heavy Carrara marble pedestal. They studied the span of the arch to be sure that its form would provide enough space for one person carrying a tray to pass behind someone sitting at the table. In addition, they made sure that two people could move the heavy lamp by inserting a broomstick through the hole in the marble base. Arco is a prime example of the Castiglionis' rigorous and witty approach to design. —P.A.

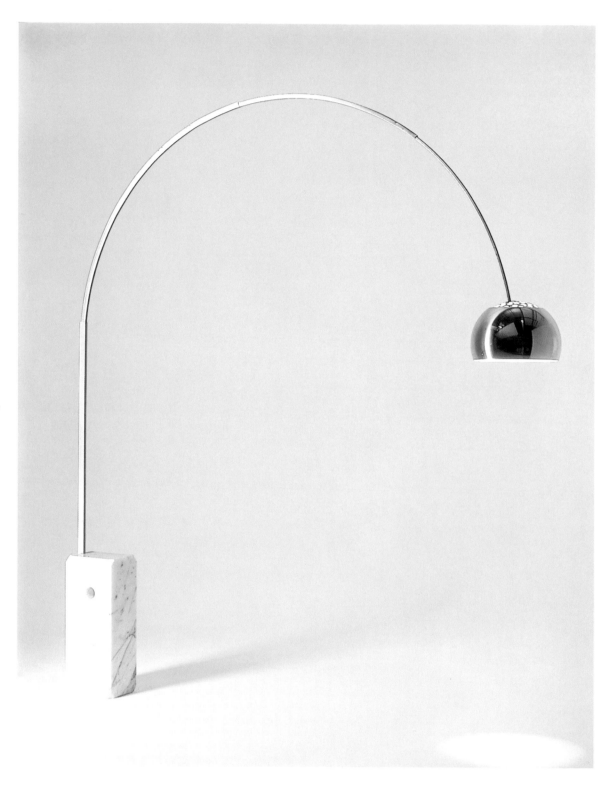

Giancarlo Piretti
Plia Folding and Stacking Chair. 1967
Chrome-plated steel, cast aluminum,
and plastic, 30 × 18⅜ × 17" (76.2 ×
46.7 × 43.2 cm). Manufacturer:
Anonima Castelli, Italy (1968). Gift
of the manufacturer

Enzo Mari
Sof-Sof Chair. 1971
Chrome-plated iron and fabric,
31½ × 18 × 20⅞" (80 × 45.7 × 53 cm).
Manufacturer: Driade, Italy (1972).
Gift of the manufacturer

Mario Bellini
Le Bambole Armchair. 1972
Differential-density polyurethane
foam, Dacron, and fabric, 28⅜ ×
47¼ × 35½" (72 × 120 × 90.2 cm).
Manufacturer: B & B Italia, S.p.A., Italy.
Gift of the manufacturer

Jonathan De Pas, Donato D'Urbino, and Paolo Lomazzi
Sciangai Folding Clothes Stand. 1973–74
Beech wood, 59½ × 19" (151.1 × 48.3 cm).
Manufacturer: Zanotta, Italy. Gift of the manufacturer

Mario Bellini
Cab Side Chair. 1976
Tubular steel and leather, 32¼ × 18¾ × 18⅝" (81.9 × 47.6 × 47.3 cm).
Manufacturer: Cassina, Italy (1978). Gift of the manufacturer

Vico Magistretti
Atollo Table Lamp (model 233). 1977
Aluminum and polyurethane plastic,
26 × 19¼" (66 × 48.9 cm) diam.; 8"
(20.3 cm) diam. at base. Manufacturer:
O-Luce, Italy. Gift of the manufacturer

Vico Magistretti
Eclisse Table Lamp. 1966
Lacquered aluminum, 7 × 4½"
(17.8 × 11.4 cm) diam. Manufacturer:
Artemide, Italy. Gift of Rita McNamara
Pleet

Richard Sapper
Tizio Table Lamp. 1971
ABS plastic, aluminum, and other
materials, 46¾ × 42½" (118.7 × 108 cm);
4¼" (10.8 cm) diam. at base.
Manufacturer: Artemide, Italy (1972).
Gift of the manufacturer

Richard Sapper claimed that he
designed the Tizio Table Lamp
because he could not find a work
lamp that suited him: "I wanted a
small head and long arms; I didn't
want to have to clamp the lamp to
the desk because it's awkward. And I
wanted to be able to move it easily."
The designer's dream lamp, the Tizio
is an adjustable table fixture that can
be moved in four directions. It swivels
smoothly and can be set in any position, its balance ensured by a system
of counterweights. The halogen bulb,
adjustable to two different light Inten-
sities, is fed through the arm from a
transformer concealed in the base. In
1972, when the Tizio lamp was first
produced, the use of the arms to
conduct electricity was an innovation
seen in few other lamp designs.
    From a formal point of view, the
Tizio lamp was revolutionary. Black,
angled, minimalist, and mysterious,
the lamp achieved its real commercial success in the early 1980s, when
its sleek look met the Wall Street
boom. Found in the residences of the
young and successful and in the
offices of executives, the lamp has
become emblematic of high-tech
design. —P.A.

215

Enzo Mari
Tonietta Chair. 1985
Aluminum and leather, 32⅝ × 15¼ ×
18⅞" (82.9 × 38.7 × 47.9 cm).
Manufacturer: Zanotta, Italy (2000).
Gift of the manufacturer

Ross Lovegrove
Figure of Eight Chair. 1993
Polyurethane plastic, stainless steel,
and nylon, 33¼ × 19¾ × 21¾"
(84.5 × 50.2 × 55.2 cm). Manufacturer:
Cappellini, Italy (1994). Gift of the
manufacturer

Jasper Morrison
Lima Chair. 1995
Anodized aluminum and polypropylene plastic, 26⅜ × 23⅝ × 31½"
(67 × 60 × 80 cm). Manufacturer:
Cappellini, Italy (1997). Gift of the
manufacturer

8 | Good Design for Industry

Just as great architecture usually has a receptive and supportive client, great industrial design needs a manufacturer sensitive to design imperatives. Industrial design is the product of a dialogue, and often a tight collaboration, between the manufacturer and designer. Some of the best examples of industrial design of the twentieth century were produced out of a strong symbiosis between the designer and the manufacturer, and many companies are notable for having committed themselves to good design. They have made it one of their highest priorities, their mark of distinction, and a valuable commercial asset.

The Museum has recognized the artistic merit of some of these producers and has even devoted whole retrospectives to their work. The first exhibition of this kind was *Olivetti: Design in Industry* of 1952, in which the Italian company was celebrated as a proponent of outstanding corporate design. Under the direction of Adriano Olivetti, the company employed the best architects, and designers, sponsored cultural and social causes, and was dedicated to its employees' well-being. The Museum stated: "The Olivetti Company, many critics agree, is the leading corporation in the western world in the field of design."

Similar accolades could be awarded today, for instance, to Apple Computer. Other companies have produced beautiful objects, but Apple's CEO Steve Jobs's obsession with good design has distinguished his company among them. The Museum has acquired objects from all of Apple's design periods, from the first Macintosh 128K of 1984, already revolutionary in typology, and the Mac SE designed by consultant Hartmut Esslinger's company Frogdesign, to several objects designed by the various in-house teams of the 1990s. The current Apple Design Group, under the leadership of Jonathan Ive, consistently produces objects of extraordinary beauty.

Throughout the history of design, a new idea or technology has often been the spark from which a great company was created. In some cases, the designers themselves became entrepreneurs. Two examples are Michael Thonet and his renowned innovative Austrian furniture company, founded in the second half of the nineteenth century, and Baron Marcel Bich's Bic pen manufacturing company of 1953.

In other instances, a manufacturer looked for the best designer to implement its own goals. One of the earliest examples of this is AEG, the German electrical company that, in 1908, entrusted architect and designer Peter Behrens with its corporate image. Behrens designed AEG factory buildings, publicity posters, as well as products such as electric teakettles and fans. His name and his connection to the currents of thought that were revolutionizing the history of design and architecture became an important asset for the company.

Germany, with several esteemed industries interested in design, has taught the world about the importance of high standards, not only functional but also aesthetic, in product design. Beginning in 1851, the liberal architect Gottfried Semper, in his essay *Wissenschaft, Industrie und Kunst* (Science, Industry, and Art), analyzed the impact of industrialization on the applied arts. Other essays followed, which invoked a conscious aesthetic effort applied to industrial production. In the twentieth century, outstanding examples of arts cleverly applied to corporate design and to heavy industry included Braun and Volkswagen, to name only two of the most well known companies. The Museum dedicated an exhibition to Braun in 1964, comparing the European company with the American Chemex to stress that a company's good intentions and hard work equal great industrial design.

Germany was also one of the first countries to understand the economic value of good design and adopt it as an intrinsic national characteristic. The most recent international mergers, especially in the automobile and publishing industries, involve the German component as the one most often used as a trademark. And every now and then surprising products like the Volkswagen Beetle are able to transcend all stereotypes.

Italy, too, is a very interesting case study. The outstanding Italian design we know today was born in the early 1950s, when several talented architects teamed up with several enlightened manufacturers in search of products. These family-based companies reacted positively both to the architects' sophisticated ideas and to the opportunities for technology transfers provided by idle war industries. Together, they established a collaborative formula, based on sharing ideals and technical knowledge, which bore fruit in the 1960s.

Achille and Pier Giacomo Castiglioni, Vico Magistretti, and Marco Zanuso, for instance, albeit design geniuses, might never have achieved their success without the particular receptiveness of the manufacturers. Likewise, many established companies that relied on big contract commissions, but also on the imitation of eclectic styles, like Cassina, would have never become pioneers of design without such designers. Because they have remained small, these companies can still produce prototypes and endorse experimentation that big multinational companies with giant overhead costs could not afford. To this day, this characteristic, together with the extraordinary level of craftsmanship available in Italy, enables these companies to provide designers from all over the world with exceptional support for innovation in design.

Other companies share the same passion for design. Some, like Swatch and Sony, are commercial success stories. Others, like Brionvega or Bang and Olufsen, rest within the confines of historical or taste niches. Nonetheless, they are united by the belief that good design is created by educating all corporate levels about the importance of design as an economic, moral, and social force.

—Paola Antonelli

Peter Behrens
Fan (model GB1). c. 1908
Painted cast iron and brass, 11¼ ×
10¾ × 6" (28.6 × 27.3 × 15.3 cm).
Manufacturer: Allgemeine
Elektrizitæts Gesellschaft (AEG),
Germany. Melva Bucksbaum
Purchase Fund

In 1908, shortly after he became
artistic director of the Allgemeine
Elektrizitæts Gesellschaft (AEG), an
electrical products manufacturer
founded in Germany in 1883, Peter
Behrens wrote: "From now on the
tendency of our age should be followed and a manner of design
established appropriate to machine
production." The Fan (model GB1)
reflects Behrens's focus on standardized parts rather than the use of
innovative form. Made from a cast-
iron housing painted green, which
contrasts with the light copper of the
blades and cage, the fan adheres to
the designer's belief that the "way in
which the outer shell is fitted should
show respect for the internal construction." Available in a myriad of

variations—on a pivoting stand, wall
mounted, with an ozone ventilator,
direct, alternating, or three-phase
current, and four different motors—
its design embodied greater choice
and adaptability through standardization, professed practical purpose
over aesthetics, and featured good
proportion over decoration.

Behrens was trained as an artist
in Karlsruhe, Düsseldorf, and
Munich between 1886 and 1889, and
then was a member of the avant-
garde Munich Secession group.
Known as a graphic designer, artist,
architect, and industrial designer,
Behrens was hired by AEG to
design its entire corporate identity:
its architecture, typography, and
industrial products. His AEG Turbine

Factory in Berlin, designed in
1908–09, is considered the first
building of its type, a frank expression of industrial architecture that
expresses the intimate union
between the process and style of
mass-produced goods, and
between art and industry. It has
long been regarded as an important antecedent of modern architecture, as his famous logo for the
company is for modern graphics.
Behrens's machine aesthetic and
his desire to awaken the public to
the beauty of his own time had a
significant effect on Walter Gropius,
Ludwig Mies van der Rohe, and Le
Corbusier, all of whom worked in his
office for brief periods early in the
twentieth century. —T.d.C.

Peter Behrens
Electric Kettle. 1909
Nickel-plated brass and rattan,
9 × 8¾ × 6¼" (22.9 × 22.2 × 15.9 cm).
Manufacturer: Allgemeine
Elektrizitæts Gesellschaft (AEG),
Germany. Gift of Manfred Ludewig

Walter Zapp
Minox Riga Camera. 1936
Stainless steel, closed, ⅝ × 3⅛ × 1¹⁄₁₆"
(1.6 × 8 × 2.7 cm); extended, ⅝ × 3¾ ×
1¹⁄₁₆" (1.6 × 9.5 × 2.7 cm). Manufacturer:
Valsts Electro-Techniska Fabrika,
Latvia (1937). Marshall Cogan
Purchase Fund

Peter Schlumbohm
Chemex Coffee Maker. 1941
Pyrex glass, wood, and leather,
9½ × 6⅛" (24.2 × 15.5 cm) diam.
Manufacturer: Chemex Corp., USA
(1942). Gift of Lewis & Conger

Peter Schlumbohm's Chemex Coffee
Maker replicates the laboratory
process of filtration to make a
perfect cup of coffee every time.
Schlumbohm, a German doctor of
chemistry who emigrated to the
United States in 1939, extolled the
benefits of filtering over boiling
because, according to him, boiling
released fats that were "disgusting."
The design of the coffee maker is
unabashedly a functional filtering
system cum coffee pot. It is made
from Pyrex, nipped at the waist, and
furnished with a leather-tied, varnished wood wrap that serves as a
protective handle.

Schlumbohm's hope for the perfect
cup of coffee did not so much lie in
the design of the pot, however, but in
the temperature of the water (200
degrees farenheit) and the filters
themselves: made from paper 20 to
30 percent heavier than other filters,
they were designed to withhold the
muddy, acidic sediment while allowing the aromatic compounds to pass
through. Brewing one to two minutes
slower than the standard paper filter,
they permitted the optimal contact
time—four minutes—between water
and grounds.

While the coffee pot was
Schlumbom's most successful
design, it was only one of a number
of products that he created for what
he called the "chemist's kitchen."
He was interested in "how things
work and how they work efficiently,"
and proclaimed himself an inventor
rather than a designer. He amassed
some 300 patents over the course
of his lifetime. —T.d.C.

Peter Schlumbohm
Tellid. 1956
Glass and plastic, 7⅝ × 8½"
(19.4 × 21.6 cm) diam. Manufacturer:
Chemex Corp., USA. Gift of the
manufacturer

Peter Schlumbohm
Filterjet Fan. 1951
Plastic and rubber composite, wood,
and paper, 9 × 22" (22.9 × 55.9 cm)
diam. Manufacturer: Chemex Corp.,
USA (1957). Gift of the manufacturer

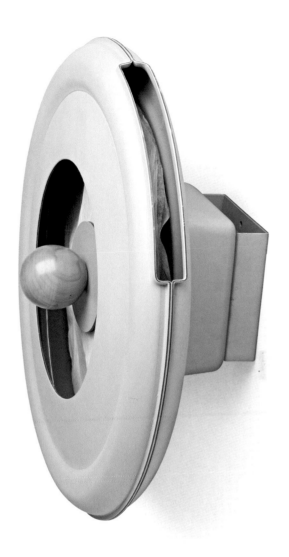

Marcello Nizzoli
Lexikon 80 Manual Typewriter. 1948
Enameled aluminum, 9 × 15 × 15"
(22.8 × 38.1 × 38.1 cm). Manufacturer:
Ing. C. Olivetti & C., Italy. Gift of the
manufacturer

Marcello Nizzoli
Lettera 22 Portable Typewriter. 1950
Enameled metal, 3¼ × 11¾ × 12¾"
(8.3 × 29.8 × 32.4 cm). Manufacturer:
Ing. C. Olivetti & C., Italy. Gift of the
manufacturer

Light in weight and compact in shape, the Lettera 22 Portable Typewriter achieves architectural balance and sculptural form in an attractive integration of protective metal housing and internal mechanical components. Sleek fluid lines and a low profile offered in a variety of colors made for a startling break from the otherwise cumbersome, severe designs of office equipment of the time. The modeled carriage handle, which opens for use and folds back for snug storage in the carrying case, was formed through a study of the direct action of the hand, as were the shallow bowls of the keyboard. Marcello Nizzoli's sensitivity to overall equilibrium in design is apparent in the careful placement of graphics and the brilliant punctuation of uniform color, in this example, olive green with a red tabulator key.

Architect, painter, industrial and graphic designer, Nizzoli was instrumental in the creation of Olivetti's integrated corporate identity, which sought to unify a progressive design program through office products, advertising, and architecture.

"Olivetti's products . . . seem almost illuminated by their exact proportions and the love with which an object should be constructed, the love with which one does his duty, the love for one's own work," declared Le Corbusier in praise of Adriano Olivetti's unique masterpiece of corporate design. The integrated approach of Olivetti's beautiful Fifth Avenue showroom in New York, now dismantled, inspired Thomas J. Watson Jr., to study Olivetti's design program in developing the corporate identity of IBM. —C.L.

225

Ettore Sottsass and Perry King
Valentine Portable Typewriter. 1969
ABS plastic and other materials,
4⅝ × 13½ × 13⅞" (11.7 × 34.3 × 35.2 cm).
Manufacturer: Ing. C. Olivetti & C.,
Italy. Gift of Olivetti Underwood

Ettore Sottsass stated that the Valentine Portable Typewriter "was invented for use anyplace except in an office, so as not to remind anyone of monotonous working hours, but rather to keep amateur poets company on quiet Sundays in the country or to provide a highly colored object on a table in a studio apartment. An anti-machine machine, built around the commonest mass-produced mechanism, the works inside any typewriter, that may also seem to be an unpretentious toy." Designed with Perry King, the Valentine is made of orange-red injection-molded ABS, in keeping with the 1960s craving for brightly colored plastics. Following in the tradition of the Lettera 22, the Valentine is more than a modern update of its portable predecessor. The internal workings are exposed, allowing access to the ribbon spools, which are two yellow buttons that have been compared to the eyes of a robot. A handle, fixed to the typewriter's back, permits transport with or without the case, which slides onto the machine and fastens with two black rubber hooks.

Born in Austria but based in Milan, Sottsass studied architecture at the Polytechnic in Turin, starting his career in 1947. He began designing computers, adding machines, typewriters, and furniture for Olivetti in 1957. An important design theorist and a pillar of twentieth-century design history, Sottsass was a founder of the "anti-design" movement of Studio Alchimia and of Memphis, a symbol of postmodern design. His humor, Pop sensibility, and unconventional style are evident not only in the Valentine, but also in several other objects included in the Museum's collection. —C.L.

Mario Bellini
Divisumma 18 Electronic Printing
Calculator. 1972
ABS plastic, synthetic rubber, and
melamine resin, 1⅞ × 9¾ × 4¾"
(4.8 × 24.8 × 12.1 cm). Manufacturer:
Ing. C. Olivetti & C., Italy (1974).
Gift of Kenneth Walker

It was hard to resist touching the Divisumma 18 Electronic Printing Calculator when it first appeared on the market. Produced by Olivetti, for whom Mario Bellini began working as a chief industrial design consultant in 1963, it proved to be enormously popular. The Divisumma 18 was small and portable, in contrast to earlier computing machinery, much of which looked like heavy cabinetry. The keyboard, with its nipplelike buttons, is encased in Bellini's typical rubber skin, which in this design is a playful yellow.

In the 1960s, Bellini began his career at a turning point in the history of twentieth-century design: the transition from mechanical to microelectronic technology. To accommodate rapidly changing technology and increasing miniaturization, new products had to be designed. Bellini was able to link the necessities of the developing electronics industry to contemporary visual culture by emphasizing tactile qualities and taking advantage of the expressive possibilities of such new materials as plastic. Bellini made industrial products desirable by injecting into his designs subtle anthropomorphic references, which stimulate emotional responses. Plastic, leather, or rubber, for example, may have the sensual properties of human skin. —P.A.

Mario Bellini
Programmable Accounting Invoicing
Machine (A4). 1973
ABS plastic, methacrylic resin, and
cast aluminum, 10 × 23½ × 24"
(25.4 × 59.7 × 61 cm). Manufacturer:
Ing. C. Olivetti & C., Italy. Gift of the
manufacturer

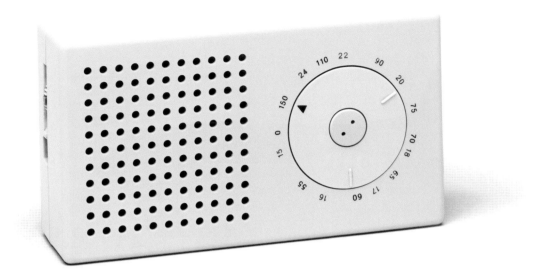

Dieter Rams and Ulm Hochschüle fur Gestaltung
Pocket Radio (model T3). 1958
Plastic casing, 3¼ × 6 × 1⅝"
(8.3 × 15.2 × 4.1 cm). Manufacturer: Braun AG, Germany. Gift of the manufacturer

Reinhold Weiss
Desk Fan (model HL1). 1961
Plastic and steel casing, 5½ × 5½ × 2¾" (14 × 14 × 7 cm). Manufacturer: Braun AG, Germany. Gift of the manufacturer

Reinhold Weiss
Toaster (model HT1). 1961
Chrome-plated metal and plastic,
5¾ × 11¾ × 2½" (14.6 × 29.8 × 6.4 cm).
Manufacturer: Braun AG, Germany.
Gift of the manufacturer

In the mid-1950s, the Braun company introduced products that revealed strikingly consistent and cohesive attributes: the use of white and black plastic, the purity of line and form, and a strict design ethic of parsimony, harmony, and functionality. Parsimony is achieved though economy of form and color, and a reduction of design to the minimum required for function. Harmony is found in clean proportions, overall balance, suggested symmetries, and meticulous arrangements of details and components. Functionality, according to chief designer Dieter Rams, is at the core of Braun's minimalist designs: "Our concept aims to strike at the heart of our product and work outwards from there. Our thoughts are directed at the ultimate user rather than at the product itself."

Braun's integrated design program is also socially responsible in its employee welfare policies and ecologically conscious production. Braun designers have often created through subtraction rather than addition, as is evident in the gap between the polished chrome of the heating machinery and the black plastic of the housing. At once subtle and intriguing, the toaster is unobtrusive, yet it beautifies the kitchen. It is one of Braun's most commercially successful designs, which include electric shavers, audio equipment, and other kitchen appliances.

Max Braun founded the company in 1921 for the production of radio accessories. After he died, his sons Artur and Erwin took over the company and reshaped its program to reflect the modern ideals represented at Ulm Academy of Art and Design. Their first design director Fritz Eichler and his successor Dieter Rams were responsible for Braun's integrated design program and philosophy, exemplified by this toaster. —C.L.

Dieter Rams
Loudspeaker (model LE1). 1960
Metal and nickel-plated steel,
30 × 32 × 12⅜" (76.2 × 81.3 × 31.4 cm).
Manufacturer: Braun AG, Germany.
Gift of the manufacturer

Gerd Alfred Müller and Robert
Oberheim
Multipurpose Kitchen Machine
(KM32). 1957
Enameled metal and plastic, various
dimensions, largest: 10½ × 14½ × ½"
(26.7 × 36.8 × 1.27 cm). Manufacturer:
Braun AG, Germany. Gift of the
manufacturer

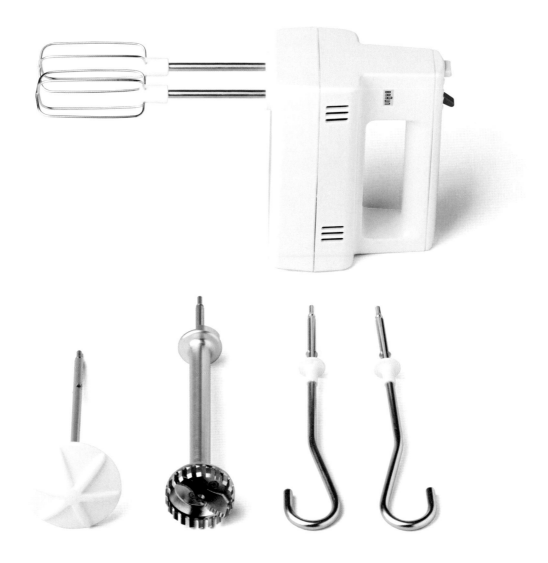

Gerd Alfred Müller
Portable Mixer (model M121). 1964
Polystyrene plastic and stainless
steel, casing: 5 × 6¼ × 2⅞"
(12.7 × 15.9 × 7.3 cm). Manufacturer:
Braun AG, Germany. Gift of the
manufacturer

Sony Corp.
Television (TX8-301). 1959
Plastic, metal, and glass, 8½ × 8¼ × 10"
(21.6 × 21 × 25.4 cm). Gift of Jo Carole
and Ronald S. Lauder

Hajime Sorayama and Sony Corp.
Aibo Entertainment Robot (ERS-110).
1999
Various materials, 10½ × 6 × 16¼"
(26.7 × 15.2 × 41.3 cm). Gift of the
manufacturer

In 1999, the Sony Corp. introduced
5,000 examples of Aibo, an
"autonomous robot that acts in
response to external stimulation
and its own judgment . . . capable of
interacting and co-existing with
people as a new form of robotic
entertainment." Aibo stands slightly
over ten inches tall and weighs about
four and a half pounds, has a camera
in its snout, a pair of stereo micro-
phones in its ears, and a small
speaker in its mouth. Its brain is actually a 100MHz, 64-bit processor with
16MB of memory. Aibo also has a
touch sensor on top of its head, eyes
that change color and flash, and a
walking pace of about 6.5 yards per
minute. Various programs allow its
behavior to simulate that of a living
creature. The first edition of Aibo, in
the Museum's collection, actually lifts
its leg to pee, a feature that was omit-
ted in the subsequent editions in
order to render the "pet" not identifi-
able by gender, and appealing to dog
and cat lovers alike.

The word Aibo itself is an interesting aspect of the design. It can be
read as Artificial Intelligence roBot or,
as Sony points out, phonetically as a
"robot with eyes." Furthermore, in
Japanese aibo means "pal." Offered
to consumers as an "intelligent and
trainable robot companion," Aibo represents the Museum's first foray into
Japanese innovations intended to
modify lifestyles, a field that has long
been of interest because of its
potential effects on the world, but
which has in the past been lacking in
aesthetic criteria. —P.A.

Siemens & Halske, AG
Telephone. c. 1955
Plastic, 5⅝ × 5¾ × 7¾" (14.3 × 14.6 × 19.7 cm). Gift of the manufacturer

Henning Andreasen
Telephone (model F78). 1977
ABS plastic, 3½ × 9 × 6" (8.9 × 22.9 × 15.2 cm). Manufacturer: GNT Automatic A/S, Denmark. Gift of the designer

In the early 1980s, Swatch revolution-ized Swiss watch design. The Swatch was designed to compete with Japanese digital watches popular at the time with an average price tag of $75.00. Engineered by Jacques Müller, Ernst Thonke, and Elmar Mock, the cost-saving Swatch was made of plastic and only fifty-one parts, as opposed to the ninety parts of tradi-tional Swiss watches. The movement plate was cast into the back-cover plate and became a structural rather than decorative element in the design. The integrated design of the Swatch ultimately had a huge impact on the international watch market.

This design took its inspiration from injection-molded die-cast LEGO blocks and from the ultrasonic weld-ing of disposable plastic lighters. It is said to have had two precursors: the 1971 Tissot Astrolon and the 1979 Concord Delirium, then known as the world's thinnest watch. The Astrolon had reduced the number of parts from ninety to fifty-two, and cast the wheels, pinions, escapement, case, and plates in plastic. Forty time- and cost-consuming operations were thereby eliminated in the manufactur-ing process. The Astrolon, meant to make the Swiss watch affordable to the average consumer, sold for under $50.00 and was completely dispos-able. The Delirium had also used the case back as the movement plate.

Part of Swatch's genius lay not only in design but in its marketing tech-niques as well. This cannot be said of Astrolon, which is little known com-pared with the Swatch. Nicolas G. Hayek, the company's president, revamped its initially conservative appearance with innovative colors and different plastics. This can be seen clearly in the Jellyfish Watch, Swatch's most invisible and understated model, and one of the very first. In addition, thematic designs and a continually changing collection of designs by artists such as Kiki Smith, Pablo Picasso, Yoko Ono, and Keith Haring, among many others, was initiated to appeal to the fashion conscious. —C.L.

Swatch
Jellyfish Watch (GK100). 1983
Plastic and metal, $\frac{1}{4} \times 1\frac{3}{8} \times 8\frac{7}{8}$"
(.6 × 3.5 × 22.5 cm). Gift of the manufacturer

Swatch
Watch (GB001). 1983
Plastic and metal, $\frac{1}{4} \times 1\frac{3}{8} \times 9\frac{1}{8}$"
(.6 × 3.5 × 23.2 cm). Gift of the manufacturer

Frogdesign
Macintosh SE Home Computer. 1984
ABS plastic and other materials,
13½ × 9¾ × 10¾" (34.3 × 24.8 × 27.3 cm).
Manufacturer: Apple Computer, Inc.,
USA (1987). Gift of the designer and
manufacturer

In 1982, Apple founder Steve Jobs sought "the best design in the world" for his company, which had skyrocketed from nothing to a $581 million market value in only six years. At that time, Hartmut Esslinger, the idealistic founder of Frogdesign, preached that "computer accessibility is a problem of democracy." Recognizing a kindred spirit, Jobs called on Esslinger to design an expressive visual code that could produce a wide range of coherent design variations. The result was a design program (snowhite) that led, for

instance, to the horizontal lines that mask the vents in the SE model. Esslinger maintained: "In computers, design isn't decoration, it's the essence." The quality of Apple's hardware design has always suggested a beauty whose glow comes from inside, matched by the operating system that design aficionados everywhere have learned to love in spite of compatibility hurdles and software wars.

Jobs left the company in the late 1980s, but returned in 1996 and resumed his search for great design.

He found it with Jonathan Ive, the current head of the Apple design department, who with his collaborators has designed beautiful objects, such as the Cube, the iMac, and the iBook, endowed with communicative skills and mesmerizing details. "Our goal is to take a great technology and make it very accessible, make it appropriately meaningful to a lot of people," declares Ive. "We try to remove the barriers . . . that have traditionally forced people to try and fit the machine, rather than the machine fitting them." —P.A.

Tim Parsey and Apple Computer, Inc.
Stylewriter II Printer. 1992
ABS plastic and other materials,
$7\frac{1}{4} \times 13\frac{5}{8} \times 8"$ (18.4 $\times$ 34.6 $\times$ 20.3 cm).
(1993). Gift of the manufacturer

Apple Industrial Design Group, Jonathan Ive, and Apple Computer, Inc.
G4-Cube Computer. c. 2000
Polycarbonate plastic and other
materials, 9¾ × 7¾ × 7¾" (24.8 ×
19.7 × 19.7 cm). Gift of the designers

244

Apple Industrial Design Group,
Jonathan Ive, Apple Computer, Inc.,
and Harman Kardon Co.
Apple iSub. c. 2000
Polycarbonate plastic, sheet metal,
and other materials, 10⅝ × 9"
(27 × 22.9 cm). Gift of the designers

n 1966, the Museum's Department of Architecture and Design organized the exhibition *The Object Transformed*, consisting mostly of art works inspired by design objects. The show's curators delineated with extraordinary foresight the paradigms that would become the focus of design theory in the decades to come. In particular, Arthur Drexler, the department's director, and the curator Mildred Constantine highlighted the emotional pull of design. They wrote: "The strength of such emotional commitment is often deplored by those concerned with 'good design' . . . Most objects occupy what may be called a psychological temperate zone . . . The emotional content we associate with any object depends on more than the object alone . . . Hidden associations may be revealed when one object is related to another, or otherwise taken out of context, or when a single detail is removed or altered. If the resulting metaphor is sufficiently powerful, even the most ubiquitous artifact may be transformed into an object of emotional rather than practical utility: a work of art." The fantastic representations of everyday things by, among others, Kusama, Meret Oppenheim, Man Ray, and Bruno Munari, revisited the connection between art and design within the Museum, and showed the need to amplify the collection's organic and modernist roots with more Surrealist, Dada, and Pop sensibilities.

Another important exhibition, Emilio Ambasz's *Italy: The New Domestic Landscape* of 1972, marked a turning point in the Museum's broadening definition of modern design. The exhibition generated numerous acquisitions, and was overwhelmingly populated by objects that certainly did not occupy a temperate psychological zone. Among them were Joe Colombo's Tube Chair, Matta's Malitte cushions, and Piero Gatti, Cesare Paolini, and Franco Teodoro's Sacco Chair, all forms generated by new social behaviors; Achille and Pier Giacomo Castiglioni's Mezzadro Seat and Toio Floor Lamp, peculiar ready-made objects; and such seemingly Pop items as Pesce's Moloch Floor Lamp, Cesare Casati and C. Emanuele Ponzio's Pillola Lamps; and iconic diversions such as Piero Gilardi's Rocks. In these transformed functional objects, the mutation, although contained within the realm of design, also had been aided by a transformed political and artistic climate in the late 1960s. Emotion had come to be considered just one more component of the design process.

Other forces intervened as well, extending the nature of design objects in various directions. A re-evaluation of local culture, for instance, had been invoked by Bernard Rudofsky's global review of vernacular constructions in *Architecture without Architects* of 1964. The late Shiro Kuramata took established rules of modernist design and filtered them through a Japanese sensibility in the late 1980s. By attacking only one variable in the modernist equation, rather than many, he created surprise and enlightenment, and he did so by learning from his local tradition. In a similar way, work such as the Vermelha Chair by Fernando and Humberto Campana was reminiscent of the focus on local material culture. Indeed, much contemporary design shows the influence of countries, like Brazil, whose design tradition based on craftsmanship and whose economy based on necessity have become important references for designers in search of a direct and honest contact with reality.

Another example of objects transformed by a strong local culture is Droog Design (dry design), the Dutch collective that has, in the past ten years, come to the forefront in a programmatic, almost political, fashion and has become the model for a worldwide trend toward simplification and reduction. Dutch visual culture had already played a similar role at the beginning of the twentieth century, and its impact was felt again around 1993. The first Droog Design collection consisted of objects by many designers fresh out of school, assembled by Renny Ramakers and Gijs Bakker, the two founders and curators, in an informal and organic way. Among the objects were Rody Graumans's 85 Lamps Lighting Fixture, a chandelier made of dozens of bare light bulbs held together in a ponytail, and Tejo Remy's You Can't Lay Down Your Memory Chest of Drawers, a dresser made of many different drawers held together by a belt, both now part of the Museum's collection.

The Museum's collection of design objects has always been inclusive, multidirectional, and subjective. In the last decades of the twentieth century, however, it has become even more so. A new sensibility that considers emotions and ergonomics to be equal functional components in design, a culture that contributes fundamental value to the processes by which things are made, the introduction of the computer, and a vast new range of materials and techniques have greatly expanded the original criteria for design in the twentieth century. What remains constant is the search for clarity of purpose and economy of means, the attributes that still characterize a modern attitude in design.

—Paola Antonelli

William H. Miller, Jr.
Chair. c. 1944
PVC plastic, plywood, aluminum,
and string, 28 × 29½ × 31½"
(71.1 × 74.9 × 80 cm). Manufacturer:
Gallowhur Chemical Corp., USA.
Gift of the manufacturer

Achille and Pier Giacomo Castiglioni
Mezzadro Seat. 1957
Tractor seat, steel, and beech wood,
20¼ × 19½ × 20¼" (51.4 × 49.5 × 51.4 cm).
Manufacturer: Zanotta, Italy (1971).
Gift of the manufacturer

Joe Colombo
Asimmetrico Drinking Glass. 1964
Glass, 5¾ × 2¾" (14.6 × 7 cm) diam.
Manufacturer: Tiroler Glashütte, Claus
Josef Riedel K.G., Austria (1968). Gift
of Rob Beyer

Joe Colombo's Asimmetrico Drinking
Glass was among the first glass
designs to break away from traditional symmetry in favor of an eccen-
tric form. It was designed to allow the
user to hold a cigarette and a drink
with one hand. The stem rests
between the thumb and index finger,
poising the cup to cantilever over the
back of the hand, freeing the fingers
to gesture or, as Colombo intended,
balance a cigarette. The base has a
mottled surface whose organic
shape seems directly molded from
the hollow of the palm, where it rests
with perfectly calibrated weight.

The Asimmetrico is a refinement of
Colombo's 1964 Smoke Glass, which
had a flattened base and short elliptical stem.

Always abreast of the latest technological developments, Colombo
experimented with new materials to
great success, especially in plastics.
His progressive solutions for living
culminated in his Rotoliving (1969)
and his Total Functioning Unit (1971),
designed for the Museum's 1972 exhi
bition *Italy: The New Domestic
Landscape*. Both projects assembled
numerous furnishings and appliances
for domestic needs into one multifunctional unit. —C.L.

Joe Colombo
Tube Chair with Nesting and
Combinable Elements. 1969
PVC plastic, polyurethane foam,
fabric, 29 × 16 × 16⅞" (73.7 × 40.7 ×
42.8 cm). Manufacturer: Flexform,
Italy (1970). Gift of the manufacturer

Joe Colombo was perhaps the most technologically inventive designer to come out of Italy in the 1960s. His innovative use of new plastics combined with his concern for man's "total domestic environment" and economy led to what is often called an "elegant functionalist furniture aesthetic," streamlined systems that could be combined in various configurations to produce different objects.

The Tube Chair is made of four different-sized plastic padded tubes that fit one inside the other. Each tube can be hooked together with any other, and in any sequence, to form a chair, lounge, or ottoman. Nested and packaged in a draw-string bag, the Tube Chair could literally be sold off the shelf. It was selected for the Museum's 1972 exhibition *Italy: The New Domestic Landscape* by the curator Emilio Ambasz because it exemplified flexible patterns of use and living and, in particular, informal patterns of behavior. It also echoed architectural objectives of the period. Colombo said: "The problem today is to offer furnishings that are basically autonomous, that are independent of their architectonic housing and so interchangeable and programmable that they can be adapted to every present and future spatial situation."

Colombo was trained as a painter at the Brera Academy of Fine Arts and then as an architect at the Polytechnic in Milan during a period of economic and artistic growth, the late 1950s and early 1960s. Initially, he was a member of the "nuclear movement" (a group of artists who saw the world in constant mutation) before giving up painting in 1958 to open his first interior and product-design studio, in 1962. During a design career that lasted less than ten years, until his early death in 1971, Colombo created over three hundred objects. In his last works, he concentrated on total habitats, designed with ergonomic and environmental objectives in mind. —T.d.C.

Cesare Casati and C. Emanuele
Ponzio
Pillola Lamps. 1968
ABS and acrylic plastic, each:
21⅝ × 5⅛" (55.2 × 13 cm) diam.
Manufacturer: Ponteur, Italy (1969).
Celeste Bartos Purchase Fund

Matta (Roberto Sebastián Antonio
Matta Echaurren)
Malitte Lounge Furniture. 1966
Polyurethane foam and wool,
63 × 63 × 25" (160 × 160 × 63.5 cm).
Manufacturer: Gavina, Italy
(c. 1969–70). Gift of Knoll International

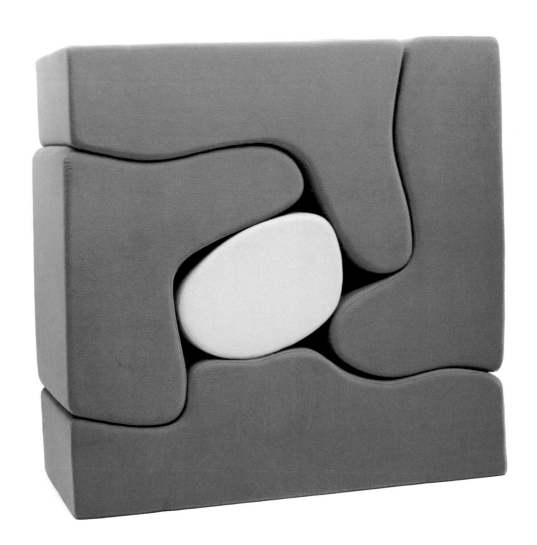

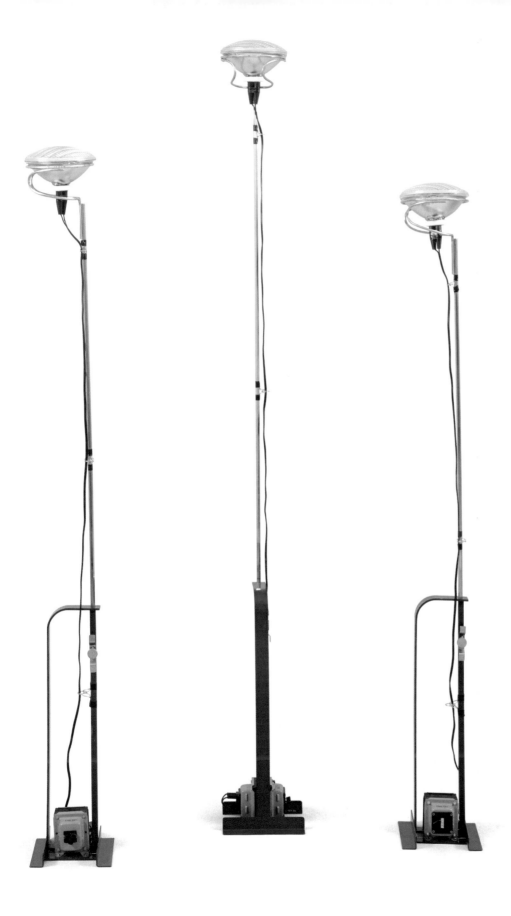

Achille and Pier Giacomo Castiglioni
Toio Floor Lamp. 1962
Steel and nickel-plated brass, car
reflector, transformer, and fishing rod
rings, variable dimensions: max.
7' 1" × 7¾" × 8¼" (215.9 × 19.7 × 21 cm).
Manufacturer: Flos, Italy. Gift of the
manufacturer

Ingo Maurer
Bulb Lamp. 1966
Chromium-plated metal and glass,
11¾ × 7⅞" (30 × 20 cm) diam.
Gift of the designer

Piero Gilardi
The Rocks. 1967
Painted polyurethane foam, largest:
17¾ × 27½ × 21⅝" (45 × 69.9 × 55 cm).
Manufacturer: Gufram, Italy (1968).
Gift of the manufacturer

The Rocks seats turn the tables on Pop imagery and domesticate natural elements instead of spoofing consumer products. They are made from expanded polyurethane, typically used in the military and in automobile production, and were introduced into furniture manufacturing only in the mid-1960s. Their painted surfaces sparkle like mica, creating the seductive visual illusion of stone. The forms appear to be massive and heavy, but the softness and lightness of the water-resistant weatherproof foam (evident once we sit down) undermine any such expectations of the real.

Piero Gilardi first came on the international art scene in the late 1960s with his *tappeti naturali* (natural carpets), rolls of painted polyurethane that simulated rocks, pebbles, streambeds, and even cabbage patches. Produced as standard floor coverings and sold by the square meter, these carpets, like The Rocks, were meant to transform the familiar home environment. By the late 1960s, plastics had made this technically possible. But instead of expressing the nature of their materials—slick, reflective synthetics—these objects returned us to a brazenly natural,

hyper-real landscape, and inspired a longing for the pastoral.

Gilardi's Rocks were part of a group of multiples that the Turin-based manufacturer Gufram produced from 1967 to 1976. They are often associated with *Arte Povera* and radical Italian "anti-design." Rejecting the functionality and formalism of modernism, they assimilate an image of a continually transformed reality, which Gilardi himself described as: "a natural environment that, motivated by hygiene and comfort, will be completely artificial, made with synthetic material." —T.d.C.

Jonathan De Pas, Donato D'Urbino, and Paolo Lomazzi
Blow Inflatable Armchair. 1967
PVC plastic, inflated: 33 × 47⅛ × 40¼"
(83.8 × 119.7 × 102.7 cm). Manufacturer: Zanotta, Italy (c. 1967–72). Gift of the manufacturer

Piero Gatti, Cesare Paolini, and Franco Teodoro
Sacco Chair. 1968
Leather and polystyrene beads,
45 × 33" (114.3 × 83.8 cm) diam.
Manufacturer: Zanotta, Italy (1969).
Gift of the manufacturer

Piero Gatti, Cesare Paolini, and Franco Teodoro approached the design of their Sacco Chair with the concept of a fluid-filled envelope. When fluids proved too heavy, they turned instead to the material for which the chair is now known: expanded-polystyrene pellets. These resembled the "popcorn" traditionally used for shipping, and were first planned to fill a soft transparent PVC envelope. But it eventually had to be produced with an opaque material— canvas, vinyl, or leather—because the transparent PVC was not strong enough to hold the filling.

The designers described their design as: "Universal. Adaptable to any body, in any position, on any sur-

face . . . an ambiguous, mimetic, antiformalist object . . . spontaneous as well as lucid, free of monumentality as well as anxiety." Distinctly youthful, playful, and witty in its shapelessness, the Sacco was, nonetheless, serious in its intent: to create a flexible object that granted the user a feeling of freedom comparable to that related to the 1968 student uprisings and the Italian "anti-design" movement, a rebellion against bourgeois taste and traditional furniture. Nicknamed the Beanbag Chair, the Sacco, has come to symbolize Italy's new domestic landscape of the late 1960s, which became more casual and relaxed owing to the influence of American Pop culture. —T.d.C.

Gaetano Pesce
Golgotha Chair. 1972
Dacron and resin-soaked fiberglass
cloth, 39 × 18½ × 27¾"
(99.1 × 47 × 70.5 cm). Manufacturer:
Bracciodiferro, Italy (1973). Estée and
Joseph Lauder Design Fund

Studio Tetrarc
Tovaglia Coffee Table. 1969
Fiberglass-reinforced polyester resin,
15 × 43 × 42¾" (38.1 × 109.2 × 108.6 cm).
Manufacturer: Alberto Bazzini, Italy.
Barbara Jakobson Purchase Fund

266

Ingo Maurer
Wo bist Du, Edison…? (Where Are You, Edison?) Hanging Lamp. 1997
Acrylic plastic, glass, and aluminum, 20½ × 18⅛" (52 × 46 cm) diam. Gift of the designer

Ingo Maurer
Lucellino Wall Lamp. 1992
Glass, brass, plastic, and goose feather wings, 10 × 8 × 4¼"
(25.4 × 20.3 × 10.8 cm). Gift of the designer

Ingo Maurer, a typographer and graphic designer trained in Switzerland and Germany, who spent several years working in the United States, claimed: "I have always been fascinated by the light bulb because it is the perfect meeting of industry and poetry. The bulb is my inspiration."

In 1966 Maurer designed a lighting fixture for an installation at the Herman Miller showroom in Munich. It was called Bulb, and it was a bulb within a bulb. It was so successful that Maurer had to go into production to meet the demand, and his company, Design M, was thus established. No matter how conceptual, Maurer's lamps are witty, delicate, and delightful. In Lucellino, a fusion of two Italian words, *luce* (light) and *uccellino* (little bird), the bulb seems to grow wings and become a glowing cherub, "because light comes with no noise," Maurer explained. The bulb remains a fundamental theme in his work.

One of his latest lamps, also in the Museum's collection, is an homage to Thomas Alva Edison, the inventor of the light bulb. The hanging lamp, Wo bist Du, Edison?. . . (Where Are You, Edison?), features a hologram of a light bulb; the material socket for the immaterial bulb is shaped as a continuous profile of Edison. Says Maurer: "I am going on and on. I never stop making lights, but it's never redundant repetition." —P.A.

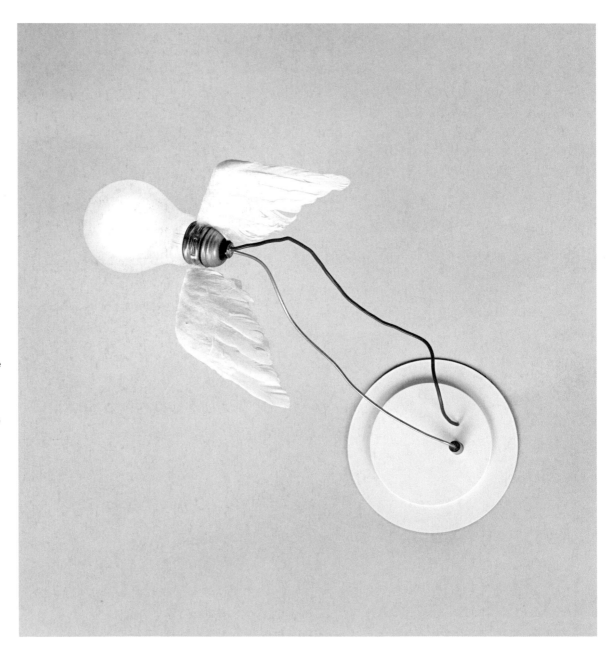

Gaetano Pesce
Feltri Chair. 1986
Wool felt and polyester resin,
50⅛ × 55⅛ × 28" (127.3 × 140 × 71.1 cm).
Manufacturer: Cassina, Italy (1987).
Gift of the manufacturer

Shiro Kuramata
Miss Blanche Chair. 1988
Paper flowers, acrylic resin, and
aluminum, 36⅞ × 24⅞ × 20¼"
(93.7 × 63.2 × 51.4 cm). Manufacturer:
Ishimaru Co., Japan (1997). Gift of
Agnes Gund in honor of Patricia
Phelps de Cisneros

Shiro Kuramata's Miss Blanche Chair
was named for the corsage worn by
Vivien Leigh as Blanche Dubois in
the 1951 film version of Tennessee
Williams's *A Street Car Named Desire*.
In this chair, Kuramata suspended
artificial roses in blocks of clear
acrylic; the flowers cast shadows on
the floor and seem to float, seemingly
frozen in time and space, free of gravity. The appearance of roses "in the
air," dreamlike, defies our expectation
that the chair, with its elusive visible
structure, could support our weight—
a surreal effect that gives the work a
feeling of dramatic suspense.

Kuramata, one of Japan's most distinguished and influential designers,
set up his Tokyo office in 1965 and
gained prominence in the 1970s and
1980s for his numerous furniture
designs and commercial interiors,
such as the series of international
boutiques for the fashion designer
Issey Miyake. During this postwar
period of Japanese reconstruction,
economic prosperity, and cultural
evolution, Kuramata was one of a
number of artists who synthesized
Japanese tradition, newfound technological ingenuity, and Western influence. He employed revolutionary new
technologies to translate the textures
and paradoxes of modern industrial

materials, such as acrylic, glass, aluminum, and steel mesh, into functional objects. These often show the
influence of Marcel Duchamp's
Readymades, the minimalism of
Donald Judd and Dan Flavin and the
playful sensuality of Ettore Sottsass.
Kuramata's poetic and often humorous pieces are crafted in accordance
with centuries-old Japanese tradition
of meticulous attention to detail. His
desire to eliminate gravity in constructions that are light in weight and
feeling has been a consistent theme.
His dedication to freedom and fan-
tasy has inspired a new generation of
designers all over the world. —B.C.

Fernando and Humberto Campana
Vermelha Chair. 1993
Iron with epoxy coating, aluminum, and cord, 31 × 29⅛ × 22¾" (78.7 × 74 × 57.8 cm). Manufacturer: Edra Mazzei, Italy (1998). Gift of Patricia Phelps de Cisneros

The Vermelha Chair, seen by some as a kitchen mop or a bird's nest with legs, is one of the many cheerful, witty, and inventive furniture designs by Fernando and Humberto Campana. These brothers are the most dynamic designers to come out of Brazil since the work of such legends as Oscar Niemeyer and Lina Bo Bardi in the 1950s. Joining others in resisting Brazil's tendency to follow European style, Fernando, an architect by training, and Humberto, a lawyer, founded their São Paulo design studio to embody a modern poetic culture in the Brazilian tradition.

The Campanas are known for their evocative, clever, and whimsical furniture, which unites industrial materials and techniques with Brazil's tradition of craftsmanship. Their products, at first mostly made by hand in small quantities and later picked up by international manufacturers, such as Edra, embody a characteristically eclectic approach to design. In the seemingly chaotic Vermelha Chair, dyed cotton cords are in truth carefully hand woven to create upholstery on the industrially produced steel legs and frame. In fact, the free-style weaving creates unique objects and proved to be too technologically

backward for the highly skilled factory workers, who had to be trained to let their minds wander.

In other designs, the Campanas' infatuation with industrial, low-brow, or found materials has led them to create oddly elegant variants on the modern chair where tubular-steel frames are paired with bubble wrap, polycarbonate sheets, cardboard, pasteboard, string, and transparent garden hoses, among other reclaimed materials. They have even given new life to pizza trays by using them as the top and bottom of an inflatable table (1996), which is also in the Museum's collection. —B.C.

Kazuo Kawasaki
Carna Folding Wheel Chair. 1989
Titanium, rubber, and aluminum
honeycomb, 33 × 22 × 35¼" (83.8 ×
55.9 × 89.5 cm). Manufacturer: SIG
Workshop Co. Ltd., Japan. (1991)
Gift of the designer

Kazuo Kawasaki's goal was to create a wheelchair that felt as good, and looked as cool, as the newest pair of sneakers. The Carna Folding Wheel Chair had to be light and easy to carry, an improvement over most collapsible wheelchairs, Kawasaki used a titanium frame, with aluminum honeycomb-core wheels and rubber seat and tires. Moreover, to offer personalized comfort, he designed optional parts that users can add to the standard frame, according to the needs of the moment. Appropriately, Carna was named for the ancient Roman goddess who had power over entrances and exits.

Kawasaki is interested in bringing technology and fine craft closer together. Known for his works for Toshiba, he pursued personal projects after a disabling accident in 1977. He has written: "Older people, handicapped and normal people are separated in today's Japan, so designers need to make designs that are kind and caring and need to treat more handicapped people equally in society. . . . To be a visionary designer I want to design products for myself first." —P.A.